Y0-BEA-485

AN ELIZABETHAN
VIRGINAL BOOK

Da Capo Press Music Reprint Series

GENERAL EDITOR

FREDERICK FREEDMAN

VASSAR COLLEGE

AN ELIZABETHAN VIRGINAL BOOK

BEING A CRITICAL ESSAY ON THE CONTENTS
OF A MANUSCRIPT IN THE FITZWILLIAM
MUSEUM AT CAMBRIDGE

BY EDWARD W. NAYLOR

𝒮 DA CAPO PRESS · NEW YORK · 1970

A Da Capo Press Reprint Edition

This Da Capo Press edition of Edward W. Naylor's *An Eliza-bethan Virginal Book* is an unabridged republication of the first edition published in London in 1905. It is reprinted by special arrangement with J. M. Dent & Sons, Ltd.

Library of Congress Catalog Card Number 70-87638
SBN 306-71792-1

Published by Da Capo Press
A Division of Plenum Publishing Corporation
227 West 17th Street
New York, New York 10011

Manufactured in the United States of America

AN

ELIZABETHAN VIRGINAL BOOK

QUEEN ELIZABETH'S VIRGINAL, AT SOUTH KENSINGTON MUSEUM.

A pentagonal instrument of Italian make, bearing the Royal Arms

AN
ELIZABETHAN
VIRGINAL BOOK

BEING A CRITICAL ESSAY ON THE CONTENTS
OF A MANUSCRIPT IN THE FITZWILLIAM
MUSEUM AT CAMBRIDGE

BY

E. W. NAYLOR, Mus. D.

Author of " Shakespeare and Music "
Organist and Lecturer
of
Emmanuel College, Cambridge

WITH

ILLUSTRATIONS

LONDON

J. M. DENT & CO.

NEW YORK: E. P. DUTTON & COMPANY

1905

To the

MASTER AND FELLOWS

OF EMMANUEL COLLEGE, CAMBRIDGE

WHO HAVE MAINTAINED

A COLLEGE LECTURESHIP IN MUSIC

DURING THE PAST FOUR YEARS

PREFATORY NOTICE

IT is hoped that this work may be of real use to two distinct classes of readers—

(*a*) Students of the history of music who have access to the published Fitzwilliam Virginal Book, but have been prevented from giving it the attention it deserves, by reason of its great size and various contents.

A collection so large must necessarily include a considerable proportion of uninteresting work. This book is offered as a guide to what is most worthy of notice.

(*b*) Students of the Elizabethan and Jacobean Drama, who daily increase in numbers, and are often at a loss for musical illustrations such as are necessary for the representation of these works, even on a humble scale.

This book contains a complete set of instrumental pieces, strictly contemporary with Shakespearian times, which are sufficient for almost any occasion of the sort, and may be written out for strings or otherwise, according to convenience.

The description of the dancing steps will be found useful for the same purpose.

As for the general object of the book, the author trusts that no reader will mistake him for a mere antiquarian, praising days long since outworn.

The Elizabethan time has passed, but its spirit is not dead; and these chapters are meant to do further battle with the ignorance which still attributes the invention of the main features of Modern Music to the eighteenth century.

The method of the book is simple, consisting mainly in a careful study of nearly Three Hundred pieces of the Tudor period, which are contained in the Fitzwilliam Virginal Book, and which, although published some years back, are still practically unknown, and almost altogether neglected.

I have great pleasure in thanking Mr C. F. Bell of Oxford for kindly placing at my disposal the photographic plates from which the printed edition of the Fitzwilliam Virginal Book was prepared.

Messrs Adam & Charles Black were good enough to allow me to use the colour-print of Queen Elizabeth's Virginal, from Mr Hipkins' well-known book, in the production of my frontispiece.

The author of the Preface to the Fitzwilliam Virginal Book, Mr Barclay Squire, will, I hope, allow me to thank him for the valuable information which forms part of Chapter II.

Mr H. Ellis Wooldridge, who was, until lately, Slade Professor at Oxford, did me the great favour to read through my work in manuscript. He, of course, is not to be held responsible for any mistakes that may be found in the book.

E. W. N.

CAMBRIDGE, *April 5, 1905.*

CONTENTS

CHAP.   PAGE

  I. VIRGINAL BOOKS—CONTENTS OF FITZWILLIAM VIRGINAL BOOK   I

 II. FRANCIS TREGIAN—DANCES—PAVAN—GALLIARD—DOWLAND .   10

III. DOWLAND, TABOUROT, PASSAMEZZO, COURANTE, ETC.   .   28

 IV. ALMAN, BRAWL, GIGGE, ETC.   38

  V. TOYE, CORANTO, LAVOLTA, GALLIARD, ROUND, SPAGNIOLETTA,

       MORISCO, ETC.   47

 VI. FUGAL FANTASIAS (ONE SUBJECT)   .   .   .   57

VII. FUGAL FANTASIAS (SEVERAL SUBJECTS) .   .   .   65

VIII. SONGS OF THE SIXTEENTH CENTURY   .   .   .   79

 IX. "FANCY" PIECES   94

  X. HEXACHORDS   100

 XI. FITZWILLIAM VIRGINAL BOOK AS A HISTORICAL DOCUMENT . 112

XII. EARLY WESTERN HARMONY   .   .   .   141

XIII. THE ELIZABETHAN VIRGINALS .   .   .   149

XIV. ORGAN PIECES, PRELUDES, MADRIGALS (TRANSCRIPTIONS) . 169

XV. THE COMPOSERS IN THE FITZWILLIAM VIRGINAL BOOK . 198

LIST OF ILLUSTRATIONS

QUEEN ELIZABETH'S VIRGINAL . *Frontispiece*

" THE IRISH HO-HOANE "

Facsimile of a page in the MS., being piece No. xxvi.
in the Fitzwilliam Virginal Book (*Anon.*). The upper
part of the plate shows a portion of an anonymous
Prelude, piece No. xxv. On the harmony of the final
bar, see p. 68 . . . . *facing page* 8

FRONTISPIECE OF " PARTHENIA " (1611)

Showing a lady playing Virginals. Observe the
position of the hands, and compare pp. 157-168, about
fingering . . . . . *facing page* 149

LIST OF MUSICAL ILLUSTRATIONS

	PAGE
Pavana. *Thomas Tomkins* .	16
Galliard. *Oystermayre, J.* .	22
Alman. *Hooper* .	31
Coranto. *Hooper* .	35
Reduction of Allemande. *Bach, J. S.*	39
,, Coranto. *Bach, J. S.*	41
Gigg. *Byrd, W.* .	43
Specimens of rhythm in other Giggs. *Bull, Byrd, Farnaby, G., Farnaby, R.*	44-46
La Volta. *Morley, Thomas*	48
Tordion (Galliard or Cinquepace). *Arbeau*	52
La Volta. *Arbeau*	53
The Haye. *Arbeau*	54
Specimen of subject and answer. *Sweelinck* .	61
Specimen of " Handelian " material. *Philips, Peter* .	62
Fantasia (extracts). *Strogers, N.* .	63-64
Remarkable Pedal. *Bull* .	65
Dux and Comes, example of	66
Subject (Mixolydian). *Farnaby, G.*	68
False Relation. *Tallis, Farnaby, Purcell* .	68
Fantasia, extract, false answer. *Farnaby, G.*	69
,, second subject. *Farnaby, G.* .	70
,, Mixolydian specimen. *Byrd, W.* .	72
The same altered into key of G .	73
Tonal Fugue, specimens. *Byrd* and *Bull* .	74-77
Variations on songs—"Daphne." *Farnaby* .	79-81
,, ,, "Walsingham." *Byrd* .	81-83
,, ,, "Barafostus' Dreame." *Byrd*	83-84

                                                                    PAGE
"Jhon come kisse me now," harmonised   .   .   90-91
"Rowland."   *Byrd*   92-93
Giles Farnaby's Dreame   94-95
Hexachords, example   100
Just intonation, specimen of possible chords   .   . (note) 102
Enharmonic modulations. *Bull*   106
Hexachord, fantasia on. *Sweelinck* 107
       ,,   other extracts. *Sweelinck*   .   . 108-109
Variation on "Woods so Wild." *Byrd*   .   .   . 113
Pavana and Galliard *en suite*. *Johnson, E.* .   . 114-115
"Mal Sims," song in Pavan form   .   .   . 117-118
"Walsingham," tune and words   .   .   . 119-120
Development by sequence (melody). *Anon.*   .   . 121
       ,,   ,,   (harmony.) *Oystermayre* .   . 122
Alman, showing key of 4 sharps and "mode." *Anon.*   131-132
"Pawles Wharfe," showing key of D major. *Farnaby, G.* 134-135
"Quodling's Delight," showing "mode." *Farnaby, G.* 135-136
Alman, showing tonic and dominant in key of D.
    Johnson, R.   137
Alman, showing Modal Harmony (extract). *Anon.*   . 138
The same altered, showing key of G.   .   .   . 139
Early Western Harmony, examples of, 13th century
    onwards, Burdens, etc.   141-147
Short Octaves, use of. *Philips, P.* 153
Virginals, compass of. *Bull, Tomkins, Philips*   . 154-156
Compass of clavier (1636) 157
Fingering of Emmanuel Bach   159
       ,,   Couperin and J. S. Bach   .   .   . 160
       ,,   John Munday 162-163
       ,,   J. Bull   .   .   .   163, 165-166
       ,,   uncertain author   164
Left hand thumb, marked 5, etc.   .   .   . 166-167
Slide, with fingering. *Farnaby, Giles*   .   .   . 167
Fingering, 4 crosses 5. *Byrd*   167
Organ music, specimen. *Anon.*   170

PAGE

Harmonies of " Veni " reduced from organ music .   171-172

Specimens of " Felix Namque." *Tallis* . .   173-175

" Christe Redemptor," as given by *Bull* . . . 176

Specimen of Bull's setting of it . . . 176-177

" Gloria Tibi Trinitas," first notes of . . . 178

Bull's setting of the same ($\frac{11}{4}$ time) . . 178-180

Sesquialtera, proportion of. *Bull* . . . 180

" Salvator Mundi " or " Veni, Creator," Bull's setting   181-184

   ,,   ,,   Bull's arpeggios, etc. . . . 181

   ,,   ,,   ,,   harmonies . . . 181

   ,,   ,,   ,,   mordents . . . 182

   ,,   ,,   and broken octaves . . . 183

   ,,   ,,   altered plainsong . . . 184

   ,,   ,,   tritone not avoided . . . 184

Blitheman's harmonies to " Gloria Tibi Trinitas " . . 185

Bull's   ,,   ,,   ,, . . 185

" Ground," with variations. *Farnaby* . . . 187

" Up Tails All," used as " ground." *Tomkins* . 188-189

Technical passages, 16th century, *Bull* and *Sweelinck* .   190-192

Madrigals, Caccini, Philips' arrangement . . 193-194

   ,,   Marenzio, ,,   ,, . . 195-196

Counter subject formed from subject. *Sweelinck* . . 204

AN
ELIZABETHAN VIRGINAL BOOK

CHAPTER I

VIRGINAL BOOKS—CONTENTS OF FITZWILLIAM VIRGINAL BOOK

THE subject of the following chapters is the important collection of clavier music preserved at the Fitzwilliam Museum in Cambridge, and known as the Fitzwilliam Virginal Book.   Until a few years ago, before its origin and history had been studied critically, it bore the name or " Queen Elizabeth's " Virginal Book, an erroneous notion having gained credit that it had been in the possession of the Virgin Queen, who was without doubt an amateur player on the virginals.   This name must, however, be entirely put away from our minds, as the evidence which is now at hand shows quite clearly that the book can never have belonged to Queen Elizabeth.

The Fitzwilliam Book is one of several well-known MS. collections of clavier music and arrangements for the clavier, which were brought together in Elizabethan times.   The others deserve mention here : they are—

1. Benjamin Cosyn's Virginal Book, which is preserved at Buckingham Palace, and has a date somewhere about the year 1600.   It contains as many as 98 pieces for the popular clavier of the time, *i.e.* the virginals, by such

composers as Orlando Gibbons, Dr Bull, W. Byrd, T. Tallis (some of which are also found in the book which is the subject of this volume), and a number of arrangements of morning and evening " services " by Strogers, Weelkes, Bevan, etc., which are well known to students of old Cathedral music.

2. Will Foster's Virginal Book, also at Buckingham Palace, and containing about 70 pieces, by similar composers, including Morley and John Ward.   Also arrangements of sundry anthems.

Several of the pieces in this book, again, are found in the Fitzwilliam Book.

The writer himself gives us a date in his own hand, viz., 1624.

It is convenient, though not accurate, to speak of all these collections of music as belonging to Elizabethan times. Although in part gathered together in the earlier years of James I., they belong in essence to the previous reign, and it would be misrepresentation to allow them to be closely associated with the Stuart period.

3. My Lady Nevell's Book, containing nearly 40 pieces, all by one composer, viz., William Byrd, who was one of the very greatest musicians of his time.   This book is the property of the Marquis of Abergavenny, and is preserved at Eridge Castle.   It was written out by John Baldwin of Windsor, who lived in Elizabeth's reign.   Several of the pieces in *this* book also are in the Fitzwilliam Book. There are some features of interest in the titles, which appear in more complete form in this book; *e.g.*, the piece called " Walsingham " in the Fitzwilliam Book, is in the Lady Nevell's Book called in full, " Have with you to Walsingham " (which, by the way, is different from the first line of the ballad as it appears in W. Foster's Virginal Book or Percy's Reliques, " *As I went* to Walsingham ");

and " The woods so wild " appears as "*Will you walk* the woods so wild ? "

The fourth piece in the Lady Nevell's Book should be amusing, as it contains a suite of movements dealing with Army Life, by Byrd :—

(*a*) The Soldier's Summons.
(*b*) The March of Horsemen.
(*c*) The Trumpets.
(*d*) The Irish March.
(*e*) The Bagpipe,
(*f*) And the Drone.
(*g*) The Flute and the Drum (spelt Droome).
    (See the "Oxford History of Music," vol. iii. p. 95, which prints a few bars.)
(*h*) The March to the Fight.
(*i*) The Retreat. Now followeth a Galliard for the Victorie.

Yet another collection may be briefly referred to, Parthenia, the first music ever *printed* for the virginals (date 1611), containing 21 pieces by Bull, Byrd, and Gibbons.

But all these are quite eclipsed by the Cambridge Book, which contains nearly 300 pieces by over thirty different composers, not reckoning the misty authors who appear as *Anon.*, and who are responsible for more than 40 pieces in this collection. Nearly all these composers are Englishmen.

There is no need to labour the point that a collection of such size, representing the work of so large a number of writers, is of the greatest value historically, and I suppose there will be no difficulty in persuading the reader of this fact. In order to drive it home, I recommend him to try and bring to mind the names of between thirty and forty reputable composers of modern music, say from the year 1800 to 1900, and then, if he succeeds, think whether his memory would serve him to mention even the names of 300 separate compositions by them!

In other words, the Fitzwilliam Book can tell us more about the state of music in Elizabeth's days than many of us have ever known about our own times. Some figures will convince the student of this.

The Fitzwilliam Book contains over 130 *Dances*; 17 *Organ Pieces*; 46 arrangements of 40 different *Songs*; 9 arrangements of *Madrigals*; 22 *Fantasias* or *Ricercare*, by 9 composers; 7 Fancy Pieces, descriptive or otherwise, by 4 composers; 19 Preludes by 6 writers, including 6 by *Anon.*; and 6 exercises on the Hexachord, by 4 different authors.

It is not going too far to say that if all other remains of the period were destroyed, it would be possible to rewrite the History of Music from 1550 to 1620 on the material which we have in the Fitzwilliam Book alone.

We may look at the contents of the book in yet another light. Thus, the 130 Dances and the 46 arrangements of Songs are mostly used as an excuse for numberless variations. Here, therefore, we have an early exposition of a musical form that was highly thought of, and brought to its climax of possibility, three centuries later, by such a man as Brahms. In the Fitzwilliam Book we have the advantage of seeing this form in its infancy.

Again, the association of certain Dances, particularly the Pavan followed by the Galliard and preceded by a Prelude, the whole forming a series of movements with a certain connection, which is observed in Parthenia (1611) and the Fitzwilliam Book, presents us with a most interesting phenomenon, viz., the origin of the suite, with its series of dance-named movements, all in one key, and subsequently of the sonata of Beethoven, Schumann, Brahms, Strauss. Here, in this Elizabethan clavier music, we see the thing at its very beginning, and we realise perhaps for the first time, that

the vile howlings and drum-thumpings of a Central African
dance of savages are in a tolerably close connection with
the refined inspirations of such poetical natures as are represented by the names which I have just referred to.   It is
instructive, sometimes, to be reminded, in the midst of our
spun-sugar civilisation, of the pit from which we have been
digged. (Any one who wishes to study this subject may
read "Primitive Music," R. Wallaschek, pub. Longmans,
1893; Camb. Univ. Lib., M.H. 22, 33.)

Once more, the 17 Organ Pieces in the book, which are
counterpoints on ecclesiastical melodies, are of interest not
solely as examples of the organ music of the 16th century,
but as examples of the stage which had been reached in such
matters as modal tonality, and other marks of transition from
the mediæval system.

The 22 Fantasias are examples of a fairly early, but
already well-developed form of a kind of composition which
we have since known as *fugue*. Here, again, we see in the
specimens provided in the Fitzwilliam Book, the great form
of Bach, in a comparatively infantile state.

Further, the appearance of such compositions as I have
referred to under the name of "Fancy Pieces," is in itself
remarkable, showing that the spirit of the Romantic School
was early present in the history of modern music, although
much hampered by the Temporal Power, and therefore
somewhat disabled.   Still it was there; and we can contem-
plate some quite sufficient instances of work of this sort in
the pages of the Fitzwilliam Virginal Book.   Giles Farnaby's
Dream, His Humour, His Rest, His Conceit, etc., are
examples, and Byrd's "The Bells."

But we have not exhausted the general views that may
be taken of this collection.   The "arrangements" (as we
call them now—the Elizabethan title, in Italian, was Inta-
volatura) of Madrigals, in conjunction with the similar reduc-

tions of ecclesiastical music found in other Virginal Books, are striking evidence that the *serious* amateur of music in the 16th century desired to have the best works of his time put into such a shape as could be made useful in his home.

So also, these arrangements of Madrigals in the Fitzwilliam Book show that the influence of Italy was being felt in England in Elizabeth's reign. The names of the original composers of the 9 Madrigals (or parts of Madrigals), of which arrangements appear by Peter Philips, are the well-known ones, Orlando Lasso, Striggio, Marenzio, Caccini. By the way, here we have dates given which are worth notice in connection with the history of the MS. itself. Peter Philips' arrangements are carefully dated, *e.g.*, 1602, 1603, 1605. This at least means that the pieces dated were not written in the book before those particular years.* Thus the MS. is plainly of post-Elizabethan origin; but it must not be forgotten that its general contents are Elizabethan, or earlier still.

Other countries also appear to have had a connection with musical England about 1600. One of the most pleasant pieces in the book is a Galliard by Jehan Oystermayre, ii. 405,† (see below); and the 4 pieces by J. P. Sweelinck of Amsterdam are excellent examples of a writer whose reputation was equalled by the value of his work. Bull, 40 pieces by whom are in the Fitzwilliam Book, was also associated with the Netherlands (he was organist of Notre Dame, Antwerp, in 1617); likewise Peter Philips, who was an English Catholic priest, and lived in the Netherlands.

Again, we can practically study the theatrical instrumental music of the time from this collection. For instance, the

---

* On this point see below.

† The references are to the edition of Messrs Fuller Maitland and Barclay Squire, published by Breitkopf and Härtel (1894-99).

Dances by Giles Farnaby, ii. 264, 265, 273,* are all called
" Maske," † and most probably were part of the music of a
" Masque."   Other pieces which might well have completed
the work are close to these, viz., seven anonymous short
dances, Almains and Corantos, ii. 266, 267, 268.   See also
the series of seven excellent short dances by Hooper and
Anon., ii. 309-13.

The connection of England with Ireland is marked by the
titles of three pieces in the Fitzwilliam Book :—

(*a*) The Irish Dumpe, ii. 236.   *Anon.*
(*b*) The Irish Ho-Hoane (Ochone), i. 87.   *Anon.*
(*c*) Callino Casturame, ii. 186.   Arranged by *Byrd.*
     (Corruption of " Colleen oge asthore.")

The last of these is referred to in Shakespeare, " Henry
V." iv. 4, l. 4, where it is spelt " Callino, Castore me ! "

The scene is a Field of Battle—alarums, excursions.   Enter
French soldier, *Pistol*, and Boy.

Pist. Yield, cur !

Fr. Sold. Je pense, que vous estes le gentilhomme de bonne
qualité.

Pist. [misunderstanding] Quality ?

Art thou a *gentleman* ?

The second of these Irish tunes, the Ho-Hoane, is a very
first-class example of real pathos, and should be heard.   It

* The Maske, ii. 273, ascribed to G. Farnaby in the Fitzwilliam Book, is
labelled Cupararee=by Coperario, *i.e.* John Cooper, in MSS. Brit. Mus.
10,444 Plut. It seems to have been one of the tunes in the " Maske of
Flowers," 1613, and in the above MS. it is also called Graysin, *i.e.* Gray's Inn.

† The accustomed order in a Maske was three stately dances, *e.g.*, as
described above, followed by " character " dances, such as of Satyrs,
Baboons, or other mountebank displays.

will be found a true expression of tender sorrow. To me the piece is a wonder, for I believe it to be about 400 years old.

The first, the Irish Dumpe, ii. 236, is a cheerful tune, by no means like the English Dump, which (according to Shakespeare himself in Lucrece, line 1127) was a doleful ditty, hence the "doleful dumps," which we still acknowledge in 1904, although they were well-known under the same title by Richard Edwards, who was born in 1523, nearly four centuries back.

Once more, works by at least ten different composers may be found in this book, which contain evidence of a growing sense of what we call Key, as distinguished from modal transition or chromatic alteration.

And again, works are presented to us here which can only indicate that the questions associated with the idea of temperament were not unknown difficulties in the Elizabethan mind. The remarkable work of Bull on the Hexachord (i. 183) frankly recognises the necessity of enharmonic modulation through all the tonalities, more than a century before the appearance of the "Well-tempered Clavier" in 1722.

Other general features (e.g., notation) might be mentioned, but as it is nearly impossible for any one to find this of use without a considerable knowledge of the contents of the book, I refrain from any further introduction, and proceed to describe the book itself.

It is a small folio, about 13 inches high and 9 inches broad, and contains 220 leaves, with music (closely written) filling up 209 pages. The writing is on six-line staves, as usual at the beginning of the 17th century.

The binding is English, of the 17th century, crimson morocco, gold tooled, with fleur-de-lis ornaments. The paper probably came from Basel, as the water-mark, a crozier-case, appears in the arms of that town.

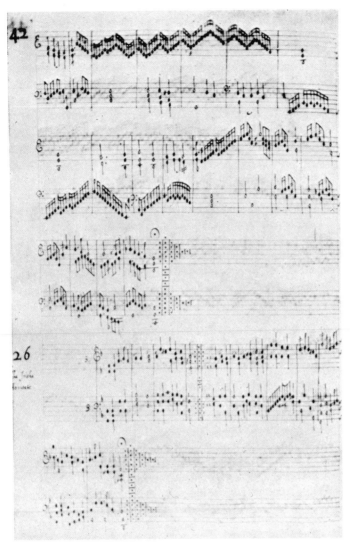

SLIGHTLY REDUCED FACSIMILE OF "THE IRISH HO-HOANE"
IN THE FITZWILLIAM MS.

The history of the book is very meagre indeed. It was written at some time between 1600 and 1620, but the earliest mention of it is 1740, in a book by Ward, "Lives of the Gresham Professors," of whom Bull was one (in 1596). Ward gives a list of the compositions by Bull in the Fitzwilliam Book, which, at this time, belonged to Dr Pepusch. In 1762 Robert Bremner bought it at the sale of Pepusch's collection (Pepusch died 1752), and he gave it to Lord Fitzwilliam, who had it in 1783. Sir John Hawkins (" History," 1776) seems to be responsible for the connection of the book with Queen Elizabeth. Dr Burney (" History," also 1776) remarked that " if Her Majesty was ever able to execute any of the pieces that are preserved in a MS. which goes under the name of Queen Elizabeth's Virginal Book (*i.e.* the Fitzwilliam Book), she must have been a very great player, as some of the pieces are so difficult that it would be hardly possible to find a master in Europe who would undertake to play one of them at the end of a month's practice." Dr Burney was exaggerating, probably having only glanced at the book, but his remark is nearly correct. Some of the pieces, in particular certain by Bull, are very nearly impracticable.

CHAPTER II

CHAPPELL ("Pop. Mus. of Olden Time," 1859, 1st ed.) suggested that the book was made in the Netherlands by or for an Englishman, and that Dr Pepusch got it there. His guess was founded on the appearance of Mr Tregian's name in the MS., often abbreviated (as if the writer knew it too well). Moreover, a book published at Antwerp in 1605, viz., Richard Verstegan's "Restitution of Decayed Intelligence," contains a sonnet by "Fr. Tregian." The name appears variously in the MS. as Treg., Ph. Tr., F. Tr.; and there is a piece by Tisdall called "Mrs Katherin Tregian's Pavan"; also S. T. is mentioned, who may have been Sybil Tregian, a member of the same well-known Roman Catholic family, who belonged to Volveden (or Golden) in the parish of Probus in Cornwall.

"Towards the close of the 16th century the head of the family was named Francis Tregian; he was the son of Thomas Tregian and Catherine, daughter of Sir John Arundell of Lanherne, and his wife was Mary, daughter of Charles, Lord Stourton. In the year 1577 the members of the Tregian family seem to have become suspected, probably as much on account of their wealth as of their religion, and (according to one account) a conspiracy was planned for their ruin. On June 8 the house at Golden was searched, and a young priest of Douay, Cuthbert Mayne, who acted as steward to Francis Tregian, was arrested and imprisoned, together with several of the household servants. At the following assizes, Mayne was convicted of high treason, and on November 29 of the same year he was executed with hideous barbarity at Launceston. Mayne was the first priest to suffer under the long persecution which the English Catholics endured during the reigns of Elizabeth and James I., and his name was included in the list of martyrs beatified by Leo XIII. in 1886. Tregian himself, who had been bound over to appear at the assizes, was committed a close prisoner to the Marshalsea, where he remained for ten months. He was then suddenly arraigned before the King's Bench and sent into Cornwall to be tried. For some time the jury would deliver no verdict, but after having been repeatedly threatened by the judges, a conviction was obtained, and Tregian was sentenced to suffer the penalty of *præmunire* and perpetual banishment. On hearing his sentence, he exclaimed : 'Pereant bona, quæ si non periissent, fortassis dominum suum perdidissent!' Immediately judgment was given, he was laden with irons and thrown into the common county gaol ; his goods were seized, his wife and children were expelled from their home, and his mother was deprived of her jointure. After being moved from prison to prison and suffering indignities without number, Tregian was finally confined in the Fleet, where his wife joined him. He remained in prison for twenty-four years, during which time he suffered much from illness, occupying himself by writing poetry. In 1601 he petitioned from the Fleet that for his health and upon good security being given he might ' have the benefit of the open air about London (not exceeding five miles' circuit), yielding his body every night to the Fleet,' and also for leave on certain conditions to visit Buxton or Bath, having of late been ' grievously punished with Sciatica.' His petition seems to have been granted, for on 25th July 1602, he wrote from Chelsea to Sir Robert Cecil to the effect that the day on which, through the Queen's

clemency, he came from the Fleet to Chelsea, he was
' enriched with a litter of greyhound whelps,' a brace of
which he designed for Cecil, they being now just a year old.
In 1606 he left England and went to Madrid, visiting (July
1606) Douay on his way. In Spain he was kindly received by
Philip III., who granted him a pension. He retired to Lisbon,
where he died September 25, 1608, aged 60. He was buried
under the left pulpit in the church of St Roque, where a
long inscription to his memory is still to be seen. At Lisbon
he soon came to be regarded as a saint; his body was
said to have been found uncorrupted twenty years after his
death, and it was alleged that miracles had been worked at
his grave. Francis Tregian had no fewer than eighteen
children, eleven of whom were born while he was in prison.
The eldest son, who bore his father's name of Francis, was
educated first at Eu and entered the college of Douay, 29th
September 1586. On the occasion of a visit of the Bishop of
Piacenza (14th August 1591) he was chosen to deliver a Latin
address of welcome. He left Douay on 11th July 1592, and
was afterwards for two years chamberlain to Cardinal Allen,
upon whose death in 1594 he delivered a funeral oration in
the church of the English College at Rome. This was
probably the 'Planctus de Morte Cardinalis Alani' which,
according to some accounts, was written by Charles Tregian,
another son of the elder Francis Tregian. In a list of the
Cardinal's household, drawn up after his death and now
preserved in the archives of Simancas, Francis Tregian the
younger is described as ' molto nobile, di 20 anni, secolare,
di ingenio felicissimo, dotto in filosofia, in musica, et nella
lingua latina.' In a draft petition of the year 1614, preserved in the House of Lords, it is stated that he had borne
arms against the friends of Queen Elizabeth, but eventually
he returned to England, where he bought back some of his
father's lands. The details of the transaction are somewhat

obscure, but it seems to have led to his being convicted in 1608-9 of recusancy, and to his imprisonment in the Fleet, where he remained until his death, about 1619. From a statement drawn up by the Warden of the Fleet Prison (apparently about 1622), it seems that at his death he owed over £200 for meat, drink, and lodging, though in his rooms there were many hundreds of books, the ownership of which formed a matter of dispute between his sisters and the Warden. It may be conjectured with much plausibility that the present collection of music was written by the younger Tregian to wile away his time in prison. The latest dated composition it contains is the ' *Ut, re, mi, fa, sol, la* ' by the Amsterdam organist Sweelinck, which bears the date 1612, while the series of dated pieces by Peter Philips, who was an English Catholic ecclesiastic settled in the Netherlands, the note to Byrd's Pavan, before referred to, and the heading of Bull's Jig,* all point to the conclusion that the collection was formed by some one who was intimate with the Catholic refugees of the period. In this respect the evidence of Philips's pieces is especially important, as MSS. by him are hardly ever found in contemporary collections formed in England. The handwriting also bears out the theory that the MS. was written in the manner suggested; though obviously proceeding throughout from the same hand, the characters gradually become larger as the work goes on. In the absence of any undoubted specimen of the younger Tregian's writing, the point must remain for the present unsettled."

Enough has now been said about the origin of the MS. and its history. All that is important to remember is, that the MS. was made by one writer, copying various MSS. of various dates (for some of the pieces may well be a century before his time), during several years. If this writer *was* Francis

* Bull fled to the Netherlands in 1613.

Tregian the younger, it is extremely likely that the MS. was written between the years 1608 and 1619, during which time F. Tregian was in prison at the Fleet, for his religious opinions.

We now proceed to learn something about the contents of the MS., remembering always, that although it was written after 1600, the pieces in it represent, generally speaking, the music of the Tudors, and by no means that of the 17th century.

I have already named some of the classes of pieces, *e.g.*, Dances, Madrigals (arranged), Songs, Fantasias (or Fancies), Preludes, Organ Pieces on plain songs, and so on.

The Dances outnumber all the rest, so we will begin with them.

The Fitzwilliam Virginal Book contains about 130 different dances, and these are of a round dozen different sorts. Most of them are the subject of innumerable variations, and thus take up a good deal of room in the book.

It will be useful to give here a rough idea of the different classes of Dances and their numbers.

The largest class is naturally—

No. of Exx.

1. Pavan and Galliard *en suite* } Pav. 26
   Gall. 26

   There are about 20 more Pavans and Galliards in the book, but independent, not *en suite*.

2. Alman (Allemande, "German" dance)   24

3. Coranto (Courante)   .   .   14

4. Gigge (Gigue)   .   .   .   5

5. Maske (meaning Dance for a Masque, *or* a song-dance)   .   4

No. of Exx.

6. Toye (of various character) .   6
7. Lavolta (the Galliard with
    "caper")   2
8. Round (Dance) .   .   .   2
9. Spagnioletta (various) .   .   2
10. Braul (Bransle) .   .   .   1
11. Morisco   1
12. Muscadin   1

                     114 + about 20 other
                    —— Pavans and Galliards.
        Rough total, 134 different Dances
           in Fitzwilliam Virginal Book.

There are, besides, others called merely "Daunce," which are to be remembered.

Some of the Dances are also songs, *e.g.*, the Muscadin mentioned above (i. 74, and ii. 481, which is the same) is known as "The Chirping of the Lark," see Chappell (Wooldridge ed.), vol. i. 177.

Again, some of the Dances were sung by the dancers under certain circumstances, and sometimes did duty under different names, *e.g.*, the "Coranto," ii. 305, is really the Pavan (altered to $\frac{6}{4}$ time) which Arbeau (1588) gives to be sung in four vocal parts by the dancers, to the words—

      "Belle qui tiens ma vie
        Captive dans tes yeulx," etc.

(See Grove, vol. ii. 676.)

The Pavan was the most important slow Dance in the 16th and 17th centuries. It was written in semibreves and minims as a rule, and was far more like a hymn tune than anything else, to our flighty modern minds.

PAVANA (Fitzwilliam Virginal Book, ii. 51).

[*Without the variations on each strain.*]

Thomas Tomkins (Elizabethan).

N.B.—(*a*) The ornaments, mostly mordents and slides, are given in the first strain of the above Pavan. In the second and third strain they are omitted, being of no real musical interest, and generally superfluous when played on the modern pianoforte.

(*b*) The florid passages at the end of each strain should be played with delicacy, so as not to draw attention from the plain chords of which they are decorations.

(*c*) The contrapuntal nature of each strain should be noticed. There is one motive running through each, in imitation. In (2) the alternation of the motive between treble and tenor is remarkable, *e.g.*, bars 3, 4, 5.

(*d*) The chromatic passages in (3), beginning at bar 4, are worthy of attention. However, this is not a solitary specimen of the kind, but will be sufficient to astonish students who may have been brought up to believe that such progressions were entirely the invention of Spohr, who lived two and a half centuries later than Tomkins.

(*e*) Notice the irregular use of the bars, *e.g.*, the two final bars in each strain contain only *one* semibreve instead of two.

(*f*) Notice the irregularity in the lengths of the three strains, viz., 16 semibreves, 20 semibreves, 26 semibreves.

Of the Pavan (commonly danced before the Basse-dance), Arbeau says it is very easy, consisting only of " two simples and a double " advancing, and again "two simples and a double " retiring. It is (as we already know) in Binary measure, and the careful Capriol (his pupil) here joins in with a calculation of the steps, saying that he makes the Pavan 8 measures (semibreves) " en marchant," and 8 measures " des-marchant."

The master also gives particular instructions about the form and manner of dancing the Pavan. Noblemen dance these Pavans and Basse-dances " belles et graves," with cap and sword ; others in long robes, " marchants honnestement, avec une gravité posée." And the damoiselles with an humble countenance, " les yeulx baissez, regardans quelquefois les assistans avec une pudeur virginale." Kings, princes, and " Seigneurs graves," in dancing the Pavan on great occasions, wear their " grands manteaux, et robes de parade." Also, queens, princesses, and ladies accompanying them, have their robes " abaissées et trainans," " quelquefois portées par demoiselles." The Pavan on these occasions is called LE GRAND BAL, and the music is provided, not by simple flute and drum, but by " haulbois et saquebouttes," and they continue the tune until the dancers have made the circuit of the " salle" twice or thrice.

Besides this state dancing of Pavans, this Dance was used in Mascarade, when triumphal chariots of gods and goddesses enter, or of emperors and kings " plains de maiesté."

On p. 29 ff., Arbeau gives the vocal Pavan for four voices, " Belle qui tiens ma vie," which is quoted in Grove. The proper drum accompaniment, continued throughout the 32 bars ($\frac{2}{2}$) is—♩ ♩ ♩ ♩ ♩ ♩ ♩ ♩ etc. He also gives seven more verses of words to it, and says if you do not wish to dance, you can play or sing it. Moreover, he adds that the drum is not a necessity, but is good to keep the time equal; and that for dancing you may use violins, spinets, flutes, both traverse and "à neuf trous" (nine-holed flute—*i.e.* a recorder), hautboys, and, in fact, "all sorts of instruments"; or you may sing instead.

Arbeau's account of the Passeměze, or Passy-measures-pavin of Shakespeare, is very simple. He says that the instrumentalists increase the speed of the *Pavan* every time they play it through, and by the time it has reached the moderate speed of a *Basse-dance*, it is no longer called Pavan, but Passeměze.

And now, to explain what is meant by Pavan and Galliard *en suite* (see a specimen below, 114), Morley, 1597 (pp. 206, 207, of the reprint of 1771), says, "After every pavan we set a galliard (that is a kind of music *made out of the other*), causing it to go by a measure, which the learned call *trochaicam rationem*, consisting of a long and short stroke successively . . . . . . This is a lighter and more stirring kind of dancing than the pavan, consisting of the same number of strains; AND LOOKE, how many foures of semibriefs you put in the strain of your pavan, so many times six minims must you put in the strain of your galliard."

The meaning of this in modern words is simply that the most correct Elizabethan Galliard was made of the same tune and harmony as its own Pavan, but with the time changed from Quadruple to Triple.

A good example is in "Partheˇnia," viz., Bull's Pavan and Galliard, St Thomas Wake (the Galliard is in the Fitzwilliam Book also), pp. 16, 17, etc., Mus. Antiq. Soc. edition.

Bull has here carried this principle of unity backwards into the Prelude, and thus presents us with a real suite of three pieces, which have a vital connection one with the other. It was published in England (1611) before Bull fled to the Netherlands (1613).

The "steps" of a Galliard are six in number; see "Shakespeare and Music," pp. 142, 143, where Jehan Tabourot's account of it is quoted.

GALLIARD (Fitzwilliam Virginal Book, ii. 405).

JEHAN OYSTERMAYRE (16th Century).*

* Nothing seems really known of this composer. I give, for what it is worth, the following statement about a musician of the same name, from the Allgemeine Deutsche Biographie, vol. xxiv. (1887), Hieronymus O. Ostermayer, described as "ein Siebenbürgisch-Sächsicher Chronist des 16 Jahrhunderts," i.e. "a Transylvanian historian of the sixteenth century," Siebenbürgen being the German name for Transylvania. This Ostermayer was organist at Kronstadt in Transylvania (Cronstadt in Siebenbürgen), where he died in 1561. He seems to have been a good fellow, and a teetotaler. Hieronymus=Jerome; Jerome begins with a "J"; so does Jehan. It is possible the two names may represent one man.

Rhythm changes to $\frac{6}{4}$

N.B.—The first and second strains contain eleven dotted semibreves. The third strain has four, *plus* eight dotted minims.

Many of these Pavans and Galliards are curiously *named*, sometimes after persons, to whom perhaps they were " dedicated," to use our modern phrase.

Amongst many instances in the Fitzwilliam Book are the following :—

Bull. Lord Lumley's Paven, i. 149.

    The Quadran Paven, i. 99.

    The Spanish Paven, ii. 131 (said to be more elaborate, and called the *Grand Dance*).

Byrd. Pavana Bray, i. 361.

    Pavana Fantasia, ii. 398, apparently so called because full of imitations, like a " Fancy."

    Pavana Lachrymæ * (Dowland's tune, see Grove, ii. 677), ii. 42.

    Lady Montegle's Paven, ii. 483,

    Quadran Paven, ii. 103.

    Others are :—

Giles Farnaby. Farmer's Paven, ii. 465.

    The Flatt Paven, ii. 453 (probably because in G minor, as *we* say).

    Walter Erle's Paven, ii. 336.

---

* J. Dowland's " Lachrymæ, or seven teares, figured in seven passionate Pavans with divers other pavans, galliards, and almands," 1605.

Settings of this tune are also found by G. Farnaby and Thos. Morley.

William Tisdall. Pavana Chromatica, ii. 278, being " Mrs
  Katherine Tregian's Paven," so called because using a large
  number of accidental sharps, the average " key " being
  E major, as *we* say.
Peter Philips. Pavana Dolorosa, i. 321.
  Pavana Paggett, i. 291.
    (Philips' " 1st pavan," dated 1580, see i. 345.)

Similarly, various Galliards, *en suite* or not, are given
distinguishing names, as—
Anon. Nowel's Galliard, ii. 369.
Bull. Piper's Galliard, ii. 242, immediately preceded by
  "Piper's Paven," by Peerson, ii. 238.
Byrd. Sir John Graye's Galliard, ii. 258.
G. Farnaby. Rosseter's Galliard, " set by " Giles Farnaby,
  ii. 450.
Thos. Tomkins. Hunting Galliard, ii. 100.
W. Tisdall (see above), Pavana Clement Cotton, ii. 306.
  Here then are over twenty examples of this custom of
naming Dances.
  Bull's "Piper's Galliard," just mentioned, is another ex-
ample of how the composers of this time would " set " a
melody, *i.e.* would "translate" it, and make it do duty in
various shapes. I have already mentioned a 16th century Pavan,
that of Tabourot's book, which appears as a Coranto in the
Fitzwilliam Book, with its rhythm changed from $\frac{4}{2}$ to $\frac{6}{4}$. Here
we have Bull making his variations on " Piper's Galliard "
out of the music of a Madrigal which some of us know
familiarly, " If my complaint could passions move," by
Dowland. It is " *Captain* Piper's Galliard," and appears in
the original issue of " Lachrymæ " (1605) under that name.
  I say that *Bull* presents us with a Madrigal in the guise of
a Galliard. But it may very well be otherwise. I have no complete evidence. Certainly the *name* of Bull in the Fitzwilliam

Book is not conclusive, for there are demonstrable mistakes
of this sort; and even the quaint case may be found of a
piece being copied twice and ascribed to different composers,
e.g., " Go from my window," i. 153 and i. 42 (Munday, and
Morley). The Madrigal is printed as No. 4 of Dowland's
"First Set of Songs," 1597. (See the edition of the Mus.
Antiq. Soc., p. 13, or the *Choir and Musical Record*, Oct. 17,
1863, Metzler).

The chances are that the original is Dowland's and that
Bull, who was the *virtuoso* of his time, took it to exercise his
skill upon. We have modern, and much more disgraceful
instances, *e.g.*, where a Schumann song appears on a programme as by " Liszt " (the "Bull" of the 19th century china
shop), or where a movement of Bach thinly varnished over
with an implicit (or explicit) melody is labelled "by
Gounod."

This being so, we add one piece to the small list of
Dowland's compositions in the Fitzwilliam Book. (These
are merely three " settings," by Byrd, Farnaby, and Morley,
of Dowland's " Lachrymæ," already alluded to.)

I shall make no apology for saying a few words here about
this remarkable man, who left his mark, not only on his time,
but upon the great *men* of his time, which is far better. Men
like Middleton, Jonson, Fletcher, Massinger, Shakespeare,
mention John Dowland with familiar affection or admiration;
and before he had reached his 47th year he had travelled
into every corner of Europe, had met everybody and seen
everything, just as did the Abt Vogler in the 18th, and the
Abbé Liszt in the 19th century.*

* The address " To the Courteous Reader," given below, which is prefixed
to Dowland's " First Booke of Songes " (1597), shows that at the age of 39
he had already visited France, Germany, and Italy, spending "some months"
under the patronage of the Duke of Brunswick and the Landgrave of Hesse,
and receiving "favour and estimation" in such important places as Genoa,
Ferrara, Padua, Florence, and Venice. A similar preface to Dowland's

References to Dowland are frequent in the poetry of his time.   One of the most familiar is in the eighth verse (l. 103) of the "Passionate Pilgrim" which is printed in our copies of Shakespeare.   As is well known, this particular sonnet is by Richard Barnfield, not by Shakespeare, and was published in 1598.

His Pavan " Lachrymæ " was clearly very popular.   As I have said, the Fitzwilliam Book contains three different arrangements of it ; and the Mus. Antiq. preface to Dowland's First Booke of Songes (pp. 2, 3) gives several lines from contemporary Plays, in which " Lachrymæ " is referred to by the characters.   William Byrd's setting of " Lachrymæ " may be found in the Fitzwilliam Book, ii. 42.

English edition of the "Micrologus" of Andreas Ornithoparcus (first original edition, 1517), which was printed in London, 1609, informs the reader that the author, at the age of 47, was tired of roving, or, to use his own words, was "now returned home to remaine," and to live a quiet life at " my house in Fetter-lane."

CHAPTER III

In the last chapter our heroes were John Dowland, composer of celebrated Pavanas, and Jehan Tabourot, writer of instructions for dancing to the same. Before we go on to other matters, it will be interesting to refer to the fact that their names were the subject of anagram, but of a different type in each case. Jehan Tabourot, being a Churchman, canon of Rheims indeed, naturally (I suppose) thought it somewhat decent not to print his own name without disguise on the title-page of his "Orchésographie" (1588), and so with simple cunning, transposed the letters thereof to

THOINOT ARBEAU
(the "i" in Thoinot represents the "J" in Jehan),

and under the name of "Arbeau" he is best known.

The anagram on Dowland's name, however, is of a far superior brand.

Fuller says that John Dowland was "a cheerful person, passing his days in lawful merriment, truly answering the anagram made of him—

JOHANNES DOULANDUS
ANNOS LUDENDO HAUSI"
" Jack Dowland wasted all his years in playing "

(referring to his lute-playing).

Fuller also tells us that this anagram was made by Ralph Sadler, Esq. of Standon in Hertfordshire, and that he was with Dowland at Copenhagen.

Dowland, like other musicians of the late Tudor times, was not only a musician, but a scholar, for in 1609 he published a translation of the "Micrologus" of Andreas Ornithoparcus (Vogelgesang) [orig. pub. at Leipzig, 1517]. A proof of his excellent general education is found in the strength and simplicity of his English prose, as it may be studied in the dedication and preface to " The First booke of Songes of foure parts " (1597):—

THE First Booke of Songes or Ayres of foure parts with Tableture for the Lute.

So made that all the parts together, or either of them severally may be song to the Lute, Orpherian or Viol de gambo. Composed by John Dowland, Lutenist and Batcheler of Musicke in both the Universities.

Printed by Peter Short the affigne of Th. Morley, & are to be sold at the Signe of the Starre on Bredstreet Hill. 1597.

TO THE COURTEOUS READER.

How hard an enterprise it is in this skilfull and curious age to commit our private labours to the publike view, mine owne disability and others hard successe do too well assure me : and were it not for that love I beare to the true lovers of Musicke I had conceald these my first fruits, which how they wil thrive with your taste I know not, howsoever the greater part of them might have been ripe enough by their age. The Courtly Judgement I hope will not be severe against them, being it selfe a party, and those sweet springs of humanity (I meane our two famous Universities) wil entertain them for his sake [D. himself apparently], whome they have already grac't, and as it were enfranchisd in the ingenuous profession of Musicke, which from my childhood I have ever aymed at, sundry times leaving my native Country, the better to attain so excellent a science.

About sixteene yeres past, I travelled the chiefest parts of France, a nation furnisht with great variety of Musicke.   But lately, being of a more confirmed judgement, I bent my course toward the famous provinces of Germany, where I found both excellent masters, and most honorable Patrons of Musicke : Namely, those two miracles of this age for vertue & magnificence, Henry Julio, Duke of Brunswick, and learned Maritius Lantzgrave of Hessen, of whose princely vertues and favors towards me I can never speake sufficiently. . . . Thus having spent some moneths in Germany, to my great admiration of that worthy country, I past over the Alpes into Italy, where I found the Citties furnisht with all good Artes, but especially musicke. What favour and estimation I had in Venice, Padua, Genoa, Ferrara, Florence and divers other places I willingly suppresse, least I should any way seem partiall in mine owne indevours.   Yet can I not dis-semble the great content I found in the proferd amity of the most famous Luca Marenzio, whose sundry letters I received from Rome, and one of them, because it is but short I have thought good to set downe, not thinking it any disgrace to be proud of the judgement of so excellent a man.

(Here follows a complimentary epistle from Luca Marenzio, dated Rome, 1595.)

Not to stand too long upon my travels, I will only name that worthy master Giovanni Crochio Vicemaster of the chappel of S. Marks in Venice, with whome I had familiar conference.   And thus what experience I could gather abroad I am now readie to practise at home, if I may but find encouragement in my first assaies, etc.

Really, a man of such varied accomplishment and excellent ability deserves to have anagrams made on his name.

Excellent examples of Dowland are his Galliard for two players on *one* lute, "My Lord Chamberlain his Galliard," which is printed at the end of the Mus. Antiq. Soc. reprint of the First Book of Songs ; also the "Lachrymæ" of which three different settings appear in the Fitzwilliam Virginal Book, ii. 42 (Byrd), ii. 472 (Farnaby), and ii. 173 (Morley).

A delightful, and I daresay unexpected, contrast to these slow mournful Pavans, is furnished by the Meridian Alman, ii. 477, "set" by Giles Farnaby.

This brings us nearer to the second most numerous class of Dances, the Almans, twenty-four of which may be seen in the Fitzwilliam Book. Here is one of the best in the book.

ALMAN (FITZ. BOOK, ii. 309).

(*a*) The ornaments are given in the above piece for the sake of completeness. In playing these old works on the pianoforte most of the ornaments may be omitted with a good result. In the Fitzwilliam Book the following sign is

used for the upper or lower "mordent" 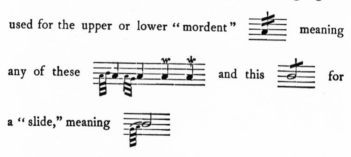 meaning

any of these and this for

a "slide," meaning

(*b*) It will be noticed that the first "strain" contains *nine* semibreves, instead of the orthodox eight.

(*c*) For the final "pause" chord, see below, pp. 95, 133*d*.

The Alman seems to have had a fairly close relationship with the Pavan and also with the Brawl (Bransle) as described in Arbeau's "Orchésographie." The steps appear very similar, being arrangements of "simples" and "doubles" (see below, p. 50), and the tunes themselves (as Morley says) are similar in construction, *i.e.* consisting of strains of eight semibreves (see below, pp. 131, 137, for two examples). Here it is interesting to recall a passage in Shakespeare's "Twelfth

Night" v. I, l. 197, where the Clown and Sir Toby bandy words about the Doctor, who was drunk some time before.

Sir To. (Drunk). Sot, didst see Dick surgeon, sot?

Clo. O! he's drunk, Sir Toby, an hour agone; his eyes were *set at eight* i' the morning.

Sir To. Then he's a rogue, and a *passy-measures pavin.*

Here Sir Toby, being drunk, turns the Clown's expression about the Surgeon's eyes being "set" so early as eight o'clock in the morning, into a reference to the method of composing a Pavan, which is *set* in phrases or strains of *eight* semibreves. A *passy-measures pavin* (Passamezzo) was a Pavan played so quickly that the steps had to be *cut short,* thus Sir Toby ingeniously twists this musical allusion into his reflections on the speedy intoxication of the Doctor.

The Passamezzo Pavan occurs under this name in the Fitzwilliam Book, *e.g.,* Byrd, i. 203; Peter Philips, i. 299; in each case with a Galliard *en suite,* which is similarly called Passamezzo Galliard.

These two examples let us a little further into the secret of the Passamezzo; for in both Byrd and Philips the Passamezzo Pavan is very similar in every way to the Pavana without any qualifying term, until near the end, where the "square" time in semibreves and minims breaks into a triple measure, $\frac{12}{4}$ or $\frac{6}{4}$. The Passamezzo Galliard likewise shows this tendency to increased speed and liveliness, for in the example by Byrd, the sixth section contains passages in a triple crotchet rhythm (marked $\frac{18}{4}$); and the Philips Passamezzo Galliard frankly ends with a "Saltarella" (i. 310), the style of which points in precisely the same direction.

The example of the Passamezzo Pavan and Galliard by Philips is well worth playing (i. 299).

While we are still in sight of the Pavan and Galliard, I take the opportunity of pointing out that the examples in the Fitzwilliam Book seem to show that only in a comparatively few cases was the Galliard *en suite* made of the same melody as its Pavan, with merely the alteration of the rhythm from 4 to 3 time. An example by Bull, "St Thomas Wake" (Parthenia has it complete; the Galliard only is in the Fitzwilliam Book) is a specially plain instance. Two others must be mentioned here, viz., the Pavan and Galliard by Edward Johnson, called "Delight" (ii. 436, 440), and by Ferdinando Richardson (i. 27, 32).

The former (Johnson, "set" by Byrd) is a first-class instance, as each of the three sections of the Pavana is almost literally reproduced in the Galliard; the latter (Richardson, whose real name was Sir Ferdinand Heyborne) at least makes a good attempt to develop the *one* music out of the *other*.

See below, p. 114, where a strain of Johnson's Pavan and Galliard is quoted.

We now go on with the numerous Almans.

It is worth noting, as a confirmation of my remark above, concerning the close relation between the Pavan and the Alman, that Byrd's "Monsieur's Alman," i. 234, is remarkably like the Pavan, "St Thomas Wake," by Bull, already referred to.

Thus we already have cases showing that the purely musical difference between Pavan, Alman, Coranto, was not very marked, although the "style" of the dancing might be and was various. Even the Pavan might (as a Passamezzo) introduce triple rhythm; just as we have seen a Pavan transformed into a Coranto on its way from Arbeau (Tabourot, 1588) to the pages of the Fitzwilliam Book; and here again we find what is, in every essential, a Pavan, appearing under the name of Alman.

CORANTO (Fitzwilliam Book, ii. 312).

[A mistake in the Index ascribes this to Giles Farnaby.]

HOOPER (16th Century).

HOOPER

(*a*) This is about the best of the thirteen or fourteen Courantes in the book. It is curious that most of them are not such good music as the rest of the Dances.

(*b*) The ornaments are omitted, except the " slide " in bar 3 of the second strain.

(*c*) The number of " bars " in each strain is orthodox, *i.e.* 8 or 16.

(*d*) The final pause chord is merely decorative. See below, pp. 95 and 132.

The " steps " of the Courante as given by Arbeau are the same as those of the Pavan, *i.e.* left foot out, right foot up; right foot out, left foot up; and then left foot out and right foot up twice over, the total result being to place the dancer further along on the floor. This was known as " two simples and a double," and was written " s,s,d." *The* difference was, that the dance was much faster. A Shakespeare quotation is evidence here—" Henry V." iii. 5, l. 32 :—

Bourbon. They bid us to the English dancing-schools,
And teach lavoltas high and *swift* corantos.

Sir Toby in " Twelfth Night " seems to regard the Coranto as even gayer than a Galliard, which again was far more lively than the Pavan. He says (" Twelfth Night," i. 3, l. 123): " Why dost thou not go to church in a galliard, and come home in a coranto ? " Obviously the journey home (to dinner) would be the faster of the two.

A capital quotation from Selden is worth printing here, which gives a general idea of the way in which the Elizabethans used these dances.

" The court of England is much alter'd. At a solemn dancing, first you had the grave measures, then the Corantoes and the Galliards, and this kept up with ceremony ; and at length to Trenchmore, and the Cushion dance : Then all the company dances, lord and groom, lady and kitchen-maid, no distinction. So in our court in queen Elizabeth's time, gravity and state were kept up. In King James's time things were pretty well. But in king Charles's time, there has been nothing but Trenchmore and the Cushion-dance, omnium gatherum, tolly polly, hoite cum toite."

Finally, Morley (1597) describes the French Bransle and the Alman as being equally in the " time of eight, and most commonly in short notes " ; and goes on to say that " voltes and courantes " also are " like unto this," but are " danced after sundrie fashions "—" the volte " (La Volta, a Galliard danced so fast that only *two* steps could be squeezed in, in each bar, and with a *high leap* every other bar. Also the dancer had to whirl round, waltz fashion. See " Shakespeare and Music," p. 148)—" the *volte* rising and leaping, the *courant* travising and running."

CHAPTER IV

ALMAN, BRAWL, GIGGE, ETC.

WE have now had sufficient description of the Alman and Coranto. The latter dance is well represented in the Fitz-william Book by fourteen examples. A whole " Suite " of them may be played from the second volume of the book (ii. 266), where an anonymous series of two Almans and three Corantos is found in one opening of the pages.

Other excellent Almans are, ii. 171 (Morley), i. 65 (Anon.), and i. 75 (Anon.). It will be observed that the general character of them all is lightness, as compared with the Pavan or even the Galliard *of state ;* and that the Alman has a " square " rhythm, while the " Coranto " has a " trochaic " measure, although the general lines of the time are still " set at eight."

A very quaint Alman is the " Duke of Brunswick's Alman " by Bull (ii. 146), which may be taken as an example of the sort of variations which the Elizabethan composers were in the habit of writing on the various sections or strains of dances. This of Bull's has two " strains," with a variation on each, and concludes with an extra " Rep.," as it was called, showing Dr Bull's nimble fingers working at one of his great tricks, viz., quick repetition on one note.

Byrd's " The Queenes Alman," ii. 217, is also worth looking at.

It will be of interest here to point out that the unlikeness between these Almans of the Tudor times and those of J. S. Bach's Suites and Partitas, more than a hundred years later, is only a superficial one. The fact is merely that Bach

38

wrote out the "variation" on his work as the original
Alman. Thus—

might well have been a 16th-century Alman, if one could
forget the positive key effect of the scale of B♭ major (utterly
unknown to the Elizabethans). And a variation might be
superimposed of the guileless sort which is frequent in the
Fitzwilliam Book, e.g.—

Agrémens or "Rep."

I will here give what Bach really wrote in the first four
bars of his Allemande in Partita I.

ALLEMANDE FROM BACH'S PARTITA I.

A similar experiment may be made with the Courante of the same work.

This is of course nothing more than an ornament on—

and so we see the *essential* features are still there.

We have traced a close connection or relation between the Pavan and the Alman, and Morley (1597) has pointed out to us that the Alman is related to the FRENCH BRAWL. We can compare an Alman by Thos. Morley himself (a capital tune, ii. 171) with the solitary example of the Brawl (so named) which occurs in the Fitzwilliam Book (ii. 269), by Thos. Tomkins, "Worster Braules." I dare not, in the face of the immense variety and uncertain nomenclature of the Elizabethan Dances, lay down any sort of rule, however modified, as to a difference in the method of dancing to these two tunes. But there is an apparently "characteristic" difference, viz., that in Morley's Alman the "strain" has the quick notes first, and *ends* with a long sound; whereas Tomkins's Brawl has the heavy accented part of the tune first, and *then* the shorter and livelier notes.

The subject would have to be treated much more thoroughly than is possible in these pages, to arrive at a conclusion. For Arbeau (1588) gives no less than seventeen different kinds of Branle before he arrives at one which was called the BRANLE DES SABOTS (p. 88 of Arbeau), the tune of which is well known to most students in one form or another. It is printed in "Shakespeare and Music" (Dent), where the steps also are given ("Shakespeare and Music," p. 147), which, as far as they go, could be danced quite well to the tune "Worster Braules" in the Fitzwilliam Book.

There are some examples in the Fitzwilliam Book of Almans

which do not altogether follow Morley's rule of " containing the time of eight, and most commonly in short notes." The particulars are here given, for the benefit of students :—

i. 75. *Anon.*, containing two " twelves," instead of " eights," but in " short notes," as Morley says.

i. 65. *Anon.*, containing two " eights " and one " ten," but still in " short notes." This is curious, as apparently the longer third strain is the result of following out a " sequence," which again leads to the weighting of the Form at its close.

i. 234. " Monsieur's Alman," by *Byrd*, which we have already looked at, and suspected of a close relationship with *Bull's* " St Thomas Wake " Pavan in Parthenia (1611). This piece is built in two " sixteens," in " short notes " mainly.

ii. 160. *Robert Johnson*, set by *Giles Farnaby*, which consists of a " ten " and an " eight," and (curiously) begins with an " outside " note, just as Bach's Allemandes and Corantos in the Suites do.

Other examples of the " outside " crotchet are, " Nobody's Gigge," ii. 162, and the Coranto, ii. 268.

A good Alman is the one by Marchant (ii. 253).

Nothing seems known about this composer, except that he was in the service of Lady Arabella Stuart, a cousin of King James the First.

And now we naturally proceed to the Gigge.

There is plenty of confusion for the student to face in the Gigges of the older days. This dance, as one knows it in Corelli, Handel, Bach, Scarlatti, etc., is generally in some sort of triplet time, $\frac{12}{8}$, $\frac{6}{8}$, or even $\frac{9}{16}$. Queer exceptions are found, *e.g.*, Bach's Partita VI. (in E minor) ends with a Gique (*sic*), in a square time of 4 minims in the bar, marked CC. But even in this out-of-the-way case, the rhythm sticks to the use of "pointed notes" (Hawkins, writing in 1776, speaks of the pointed note, meaning "dotted," and says there was no authority for a Jigg having this as a general feature).

All I know about the history of the Jig is in my book, "Shakespeare and Music," pp. 124, 125, and 117, with the two examples on p. 205.

A GIGG (Fitzwilliam Book, ii. 237).

WILLIAM BYRD, 1538-1623.

WILLIAM BYRD.

(*a*) The solitary ornament given in the MS. of this piece is printed above, in bar 1.

(*b*) The two strains are plainly meant to "repeat." See the final crotchet preceding the first double bar, and the two quavers in the bar preceding the "pause chord" at the end, which clearly lead back to the repetition of strain 2.

(*c*) Something seems wanting in bars 6 and 10.

(*d*) The inquiring student will rejoice to find several consecutive fifths in three consecutive bars.

But the very various rhythms and times of the Gigges in the Fitzwilliam Book are worth looking at. All the five instances are in the second volume, and I will here give examples of their rhythm formulas.

Thus, whereas the "Cobbler's Jig" (1622), and Bull's "King's Hunting Jig" (1580 or later) are in 4 time, and have no suspicion of triplets in them, we find that in the 18th century (Bach, etc.), the Gigue seems to have taken the triplet rhythm as its principal characteristic.

The examples in the Fitzwilliam Book are as follows :—

ii. 257—"DOCTOR BULL'S *MYSELFE*"—GIGGE.

Time   *Rhythmical Scheme.*

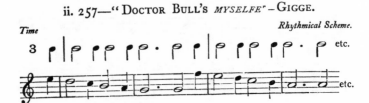

ii. 258—(Also by BULL).

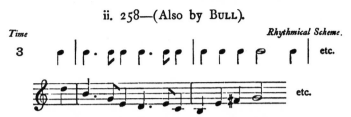

This latter is a curious experiment in mixed rhythm, quite in Bull's characteristic manner, and is worth playing.

ii. 237—WILLIAM BYRD— (with F. Tr. in margin).

ii. 416—GILES FARNABY—A very curious case in two ways :
(*a*) It is in 4 time, and
(*b*) The strains are built in *Nines*, not "eights."

There are four sections of this Gigge, and all of the last three are variations on No. 1.

ii. 162.— RICHARD FARNABY. — "Nobody's Gigge." A good tune.

in "eights," with an "outside" crotchet (see above).

Richard Farnaby was the son of Giles.

The Farnabys came from Cornwall, and therefore Mr Tregian may have known them personally. At any rate there are 50 pieces by the father, and 4 by the son, in the Fitzwilliam Book.

Giles Farnaby took his Mus. B. degree at Oxford, from Christ Church, in 1592, and in his "supplicat" stated that he had studied music for twelve years.

Twenty-nine years later (1621), he was one of the contributors to the harmonised tunes in Ravenscroft's Psalter.

I have more to say about the Farnabys, which must be put off till a later occasion.

Both Giles (the father) and Richard (the son) were persons of great gifts, and are certainly amongst the most important of the authors represented in the Fitzwilliam Book.

CHAPTER V

TOYE, CORANTO, LAVOLTA, GALLIARD, ROUND, SPAGNIOLETTA, MORISCO, ETC.

I HAVE mentioned the small class of dance pieces called "Toye." There are six pieces given with this name; one has been already spoken of, as it appears in two places (ii. 260, "Toye," and ii. 267, "Coranto"), there being slight differences between the copies, which seem to show that Mr Tregian did not recognise the piece, as he reproduced it almost immediately under the name of Coranto. It is pretty certain that he must have had it in *two* MSS., from different sources.

But other examples are to hand, ii. 412 and 413, which make it clear that a "Toye" need not be a Coranto, nor a Coranto a "Toye." Both these pieces are *called* "Toye," but the one (Duchesse of Brunswick's Toye, by Bull) is in $\frac{6}{4}$ time, the other (*Anon.*) in quadruple time.

Both are worth playing. The harmony of the second strain of the *Anon.* "Toye," ii. 413, is remarkable : ii. 421 contains a "Toye" by Giles Farnaby, the first strain of which is practically the same as Bull's "Duchesse of Brunswick," and on the whole is a better piece than Bull's.

Here we may consider a particularly charming and beautiful Galliard by Giles Farnaby (ii. 419), which happens to be copied into the Fitzwilliam Book alongside of these "Toyes." It consists of the usual three strains, beginning with a sweet melody in A minor, which is not at all unlike what Rameau (1683-1764) would write, more than a century later. The third strain (p. 420) is very remarkable for the beauty of the antiphonal use of the two hands.

We now proceed with miscellaneous Dances, such as the Lavolta, Round, Spagnioletta, Morisco, and Muscadin.

LA VOLTA (*Lavolte*), FITZWILLIAM BOOK, ii. 188.

[*The quick-time Galliard.*]

THOMAS MORLEY (1563-1604).
Set by W. BYRD.

The variations on the two strains are omitted.

In connection with the two Lavoltas (both by Byrd) found in the Fitzwilliam Book, I will say a few words about the class of triple-time Dances, of which the Lavolta is one.

The father and mother of all these trochaic Dances is the

BASSE Dance, of the 15th century.   (" Basse " means *par bas*, *i.e.* sliding along the ground.)

I here quote from " Shakespeare and Music " Arbeau's account of this Dance, as it is given in " Orchésographie " (1588) :—

" On p. 25, Capriol (the Pupil) asks his Master (Arbeau) to describe the steps of the 'basse' dance. This was the 'danse par bas, ou sans sauter,' which was of the 15th century, was in triple time, and contained three parts, A, basse dance; B, Retour de la basse dance; C, Tordion. This third part, or tordion, 'n'est aultre chose qu'une gaillarde *par terre*'; *i.e.* the Tordion of a Basse dance was simply a Galliard *par terre*, without the leaping or 'Sault majeur.'

" Before Arbeau answers his pupil, he gives him some preliminary instruction as to the etiquette of the ball-room. He says—' In the first place . . . you should choose some virtuous damsel whose appearance pleases you (telle que bon vous semblera), take off your hat or cap in your left hand, and tender her your right hand to lead her out to dance. She, being modest and well brought up, will give you her left hand, and rise to follow you. Then conduct her to the end of the room, face each the other, and tell the band to play a basse dance. For if you do not, they may inadvertently play some other kind of dance. And when they begin to play, you begin to dance.'

" *Capriol.* If the lady should refuse, I should feel dreadfully ashamed.

" *Arbeau.* A properly educated young lady NEVER refuses one who does her the honour to lead her out to the dance. If she does, she is accounted foolish (sotte), for if she doesn't want to dance, what is she sitting there for amongst the rest ?

" The Master then gives his pupil an account of the basse

dance, the 1st and 2nd parts of which are composed of
various arrangements of the following movements—

1. La révérence, marked with a big R.
2. Le branle (*not* the dance of that name), marked with b.
3. Deux simples, marked ss.
4. Le double, marked d.
5. La reprise, marked with a little r.

" The 'chanson'—*i.e.* the dance tune, was played on the
flute, and accompanied by the 'tabourin' or drum, which
beats all the time.   Every 'bar' of the music is called
either a 'battement' of the drum, or a 'mesure' of the
chanson.

" Now Arbeau explains the steps and time of each of the
above five movements.

" 1. R. This takes four bars. Begin with left foot forward,
and in doing the révérence, half turn your body and face
towards the Damoiselle, and cast on her 'un gracieux
regard.'

" 2. b.* Also takes four bars. Keep the feet joined together,
then for the first bar, swing the body gently to the left side;
second bar, swing to the right, while gazing modestly upon
' les assistants'; third bar, swing again to the left; and
for the fourth bar, swing to the right side, looking on the
Damoiselle with an 'oeillade defrobée, doulcement et
discretement.'

" 3. ss. 1st bar, left foot forward; 2nd bar, bring right
foot up to the said left foot; 3rd bar, advance the right
foot; 4th bar, join the left foot to the said right foot; et
ainsi sera parfaict le mouvement des deux simples.

" *N.B.*—Always suit the length of your steps to the size of

---

* The branle (not the dance, but as used here) is called *Congedium* by
Anthoine Arena. Arbeau thinks because the dancer appears about to take
leave of his partner—*i.e. prendre congé.* See Hen. VIII., iv. 2. l. 82, stage
direction, " congee."

the room, and the convenience of the Damoiselle, who cannot with modesty take such big steps as you can.

"4. d. 1st bar, advance left foot; 2nd, advance right foot; 3rd, advance left foot; 4th, join right to left. For *two* doubles (dd) do it over again, but contrariwise, beginning with the Right foot. For *three* doubles (ddd), the form of the third will be, 1st bar, advance left foot; 2nd, advance right foot; 3rd, advance left foot; 4th, 'puis tumberà pieds joincts comme a estè faict au premier double.' And thus (he carefully adds) the three doubles are achieved in 12 'battements et mesures du tabourin.'

"5. The Reprise (r) is commonly found before the branle (b), and sometimes before the double (d) [see the Memoires]. In it you have to cultivate a certain movement of the knees, or feet, or 'les artoils seullement,' as if your feet were shaking under you. 1st bar, 'les artoils' of the right foot; 2nd bar, do.; 3rd bar, of the left foot; 4th, of the right foot again.

"The *Memoire* of the movements of the basse dance—*i.e.* its first Part, is—

R b ss d r | d r b ss ddd r d r b | ss d r b C.

The C means the 'congé,' or 'leave' which you must take of the Damoiselle; salute her, and keep hold of her hand, and lead her back to where you began, in order to dance the Second Part—namely, the Retour de la basse dance, the *Memoire* for which is—

b | d r b ss ddd r d r b | C.

[The nine movements enclosed between the upright lines, are the same in both parts.]

"Capriol now remarks that he has been counting up, and finds that the music of the *basse dance* proper (part 1) has 20 'fours' (vingt quaternions), and the *retour* (part 2) has 12 'fours.'

"Arbeau then describes the Tordion, which is Part 3 of the

basse dance. He says it is still in triple time, but plus legiere et concitée,' and does not consist of 'simples, doubles, reprises,' etc., like the first and second parts, but is danced almost exactly as a Galliard, except that it is *par terre*—*i.e.* without any capers, and low on the ground, with a quick and light step; whereas the Galliard is danced *high*, with a slower and weightier 'mesure.'

"He gives the following tune, which will fit to *any* of the innumerable diversities of Galliard. If played fast, it is a Tordion, if slower, a Galliard. [There are, of course, no bars in the original.]

TORDION OR GALLIARD (CINQUEPACE).

"Here are the Steps of the Galliard, consisting of five movements of the feet, and the caper, or 'sault majeur.' The five steps give the Galliard the name of Cinque pas.

  I. Greve gaulche. ['Greve' is explained as a 'coup de pied.']

  2. Greve droicte.

  3. ,,   gaulche.

  4. ,,   droicte.

  5. Sault majeur.

  6. Posture gaulche.

"1, 2, 3, 4, 6, are the 'Cinq' pas, and 5 is the characteristic leap or caper.

" The next six minims are danced to the Revers, which is just the same, except that the words ' right' and ' left ' (*droicte* and *gaulche*) change places all the way down. Then repeat till the tune is finished.

AIR D'UNE VOLTE. [LA VOLTA.]

1. Petit pas, en saultant sur le gaulche, pour faire pied en l'air droit.
2. Plus grand pas du droit.
3. Sault majeur.
4. Posture en pieds joincts ;
    etc., all over again every two bars.

" The sault majeur of the ' high lavolt' comes at the semibreves in this tune."

Thus, the Tordion is Part III. of the BASSE Dance, which was *par terre*. The Galliard is the Tordion with the sault majeur or " leap " or " caper." The Volta (Lavolt) is the Galliard cut short as to its steps, and with most of the importance laid on the " caper," which was " high " (see " Twelfth Night "), and adorned with a whirling movement in addition. (See ii. 180, 188, for Lavoltas by William Byrd. The tune of the latter is by Thomas Morley.)

The Round. i. 248, Byrd's " Sellinger's Round," also called " The Beginning of the World." Chappell, vol. i. 256.

[Sellinger = St Leger (not far from Cornwall again.)]

And ii. 292, Byrd's " Gipsy's Round."

Both are in $\frac{6}{4}$, and with ♩ ♪♩ as a characteristic.

Both are worth playing. The former has a curious likeness to a well-known hymn tune, " St Theodulph." (See the
S. John Passion, No. 28.   Date about 1725.)

All that seems known about the Dancing of the Round is,
that it has some relation to the Hay, or Raye, which was
popular both in England and France in the 16th century.

Haie means Hedge in French, and " faire la haie" seems to
be explainable as follows :—

Arbeau says—first the dancers dance alone, each separately ;
then together *so as to interlace*, " et font *la haye* les uns parmy
les aultres."   That is, during each batch of four steps, the
dancers *change places* one with another, so that if there are
three dancers, A, B, C, in the first four steps, B and A
change places, and make B, A, C ; in the next four steps, C
and A change places, and make B, C, A, etc.

Here is the tune and the formula of steps—

THE HAYE

Beginning at the first complete bar, and reckoning one
step to each semibreve—1. Deux simples (ss).   2. Double
(d).   3. ss.   4. d.   5. ss.   6. d.   7. ss.   8. d.

The formula of steps ss d ss d (repeat) would at all events carry the dancers " round " the room.

The Spagnioletta, of which there are two examples, i. 199, by Giles Farnaby, and ii. 471 (the *Old* Spagnoletta) by the same. The first is in 4 time, but the second in triple, besides showing a very strong family likeness to the " Sellinger's Round."

We now come to the

Morisco, ii. 373, a solitary but excellent specimen in the Fitzwilliam Book. *Anon.*, and called " The King's Morisco." It has six short strains, which admirably illustrate the immense difference between the key effect of our modern Scales and that of the old Modes; some of them ending on a chord of C major, others (of course) on a chord of A major. The square time continues until the sixth section, when $\frac{12}{4}$ time begins.

Other Moriscos with which these may be compared are in " Shakespeare and Music," p. 151, Arbeau's tune (the steps given seem to bring the Morisco very near to the modern clog dances of the music-hall), and the Moresca of Monteverde (Orfeo, 1608), the latter being all through in triple time (" Shakespeare and Music," p. 206).

This last is a very ingenious piece, as it consists simply of 8 bars (or 4, according to the barring), which are repeated in 4 different keys, so as to produce 32 bars of music out of the same phrase; and it manages to finish the fourth repetition on the same chord on which the first begins: so the dance can be repeated *ad placitum*.

The Muscadin, i. 74 and ii. 481 (which gives variations on the same tune by Giles Farnaby), is not unlike the accepted Hornpipe tunes. This particular example (a solitary one) is found in Chappell's "Popular Music of the Olden Time" under the name of " The Chirping of the Lark " (Wooldridge's ed., vol. i. p. 277), and thus furnishes us with one of the many cases where a dance tune is used as a song, or *vice versâ*.

I will close my account of the numerous Dances of the Fitzwilliam Book by referring to some of the best examples which are contained in this work.

Pavana by W. Byrd, ii. 384.

Galliard by J. Oystermayre, ii. 405 (see above, p. 22).

Pavana by Thomas Tomkins, ii. 51 (best played without *agrémens*, see above, p. 16).

Galliard by Thomas Morley (ii. 177).

Two Almans by Robert Johnson, ii. 158, 159 (see below, p. 137).

Coranto, *Anon.*, ii. 310.

CHAPTER VI

Up to this point we have tried (and, of course, failed) to deal completely with the Dances of the Fitzwilliam Virginal Book. We have seen something at least of about a dozen sorts of dance tunes which were current in Elizabethan times ; and made some inroads amongst the 130 to 140 different examples of these which are preserved in this one book alone.

We still have before us the consideration of 46 Songs, 17 Organ Pieces, 9 arrangements of Madrigals, 22 Fantasias, 7 "Romantic" Pieces, 19 Preludes, and the important class of 6 works on the Hexachord, besides the general questions concerning Tonality, Acoustical Temperament, Musical Form, and other historical matters, which can all receive light from a careful study of the nearly 300 pieces in this volume. Furthermore, at least 28 different composers whose names and works appear in the Fitzwilliam Book must have some notice given to them of a directly personal kind, and some attempt must be made to appreciate and compare the various features of their compositions.

I have already pointed out that in the Fitzwilliam Book various "forms" of our modern music are to be seen in their infancy, and that this circumstance alone would make the book invaluable to the student, *e.g.*, in Chapter I., where the "variation form" of the 16th century was brought before the reader. Numberless "variations" on Elizabethan songs and dances occupy a large proportion of the pages of the Fitzwilliam Book. Specimens are given below, pp. 79-84. We will now proceed to the examples of another form of modern music which can be studied in an early stage in the Fitzwilliam Book, viz., that of Fugue.

The thing called Fugue existed in the 16th century under the name Fantasia, or Ricercare. The name "Fancy" was common in England in the 17th century, *i.e.* "Fantasia" anglicised. The Ricercare was simply a more *elaborate* example of fugal writing, and its name ("sought out," *recherché*, exquisite) merely indicates that every possible contrapuntal ingenuity would be exhibited. But the names were used with no particular care, and in any case the great point to remember is, that both practically mean "Fugue"; but "Fugue" as it was practised a hundred years before J. S. Bach was even born. The word "Fugue" in the 16th century did not indicate what is now understood by the term. When Morley (1597) gives us an example of what he calls a Fugue, it turns out to be what we describe as a Canon, or Imitation.

So, some time between 1600 and 1700, the name of these contrapuntal works was changed from Fantasia or Ricercar to the name of Fugue, which was certainly used in Germany during the latter years of the 17th century (Buxtehude), and in England earlier still, viz., in 1665, when John Milton used the term in the Eleventh Book of "Paradise Lost."

> "the sound
> Of instruments that made melodious chime
> Was heard, of harp and organ; and who moved
> Their stops and chords was seen; his volant touch,
> Instinct through all proportions low and high,
> Fled and pursued transverse the resonant fugue."

Almost all the best music of the 16th and 17th centuries,

except the single-voice songs, or duet dialogues, or dances, was fugal. Whether vocal or instrumental, the "form" of part music was practically only one, that of the fugal Fantasia or Ricercar. The church music for voices, or the chamber music for viols, were not only singularly alike in general tone, but were most usually constructed in the same way, *i.e.* the fugal way. There might be *one* subject, or several, or a large number, introduced in turn, either singly or in combination with others; but the general plan was that known as Fantasia; and that, again, was in its principal features almost the same as what has been known, now for two hundred years, to musicians as FUGUE.

We shall find it interesting, both musically and historically, to examine in some detail a few of these older examples of Fugue taken from the Fitzwilliam Virginal Book, which contains twenty-two of them, by eight different composers, who were all living at the same time as William Shakespeare. It is worth remembering here, that, although Shakespeare uses musical terms with such familiarity, he never mentions the word Fugue; but he does refer to the musical form we are considering, under the term we should expect, viz., Fancy—in the second part of "Henry IV." iii. 2, l. 320, where Falstaff meditates on Mr Shallow's lies about his wildness in early youth.

Fal. He [Shallow] came ever in the rearward of the fashion, and sung those tunes . . . that he heard the carmen whistle, and sware—they were his *fancies*, or his *good nights* . . . etc."

The same kind of music is referred to in "Cymbeline," ii. 3, l. 11, where Cloten provides instrumental and vocal music as a serenade to Imogen, and asks for two pieces :—

" First, a very excellent good-conceited thing: after, a wonderful sweet air, with admirable rich words to it."

This "good-conceited thing" is nothing else than a "Fancy"

or "Ricercar" for viols, and is aptly described by Cloten, being made always as full of "good conceits" (*i.e.* contrapuntal tricks, as of diminution, augmentation, imitation, answer *per Arsin et Thesin,* or *Recte et Retro,* etc.) as it would hold, or as the ability of the composer would permit.

The names of the composers of such pieces as this, which are found in the Fitzwilliam Book, are: Bull, Byrd, Giles Farnaby, Morley, John Munday, Peter Philips, Nic. Strogers, and J. P. Sweelinck, the Dutchman. (The index of the printed Fitzwilliam Book credits W. Tisdall with a Fantasia. This is merely a mistake for Tisdall's Galliard, ii. 486.)

All are English except Sweelinck of Amsterdam, who is connected with two of the others, Bull and Philips, in a peculiar way, for Bull at one period of his life lived in Antwerp, being organist of Notre Dame there in 1617; and Philips, an English Catholic priest, also lived in the Netherlands.

We will make a good beginning of this subject by studying Sweelinck's Fantasia in ii. 297 of the Fitzwilliam Virginal Book, and a Fantasia by Philips, i. 335, both of which exhibit some of the most characteristic features of this "form" as it was practised in England, Italy, and the Netherlands (not to mention Germany), in the latter part of the 16th century.

Both these works are lengthy, and might, with some justice, be called "dull"; but there is no doubt of their historical value, and I imagine it is very largely the change in the mental attitude of modern audiences that denies such music its artistic success. However that may be, let us look at them with reverent interest as examples of the practice of the older method of contrapuntal writing which made J. S. Bach a possibility, and (finally) an actual master in this kind.

These two Fantasias (Dutch and English) have more than

one thing in common besides their great length. Both have *one main subject*, and they stick to that one subject in an admirable way.

Both works are written for a keyed instrument, *e.g.*, the harpsichord or organ, whereas many works of the sort were scored for strings or wind.

Both of them are full of the quaint conceits alluded to above, presenting the subject in Imitation by direct motion, by contrary motion, by augmentation, by diminution, by double diminution (*i.e.* the subject introduced in notes of a quarter the original length), in stretto, and in combination with subsidiary motives.

Both of them are true Fantasias, as they are built on original subjects, not on ecclesiastical plain-songs.

Here is the "subject" of Sweelinck's Fantasia, together with its "answer" in contrary motion.

J. P. SWEELINCK.

[*Answer in Contrary Motion.*]

This subject is a long one, and the very first thing Sweelinck does is to give the whole of it in "answer" by contrary motion, at the distance of a single bar (ii. 297, line 1).

On line 4 an episodic passage begins, and the Fantasia is fairly under way.

Some of the "scientific" features are: Page 298, bottom line, subject by augmentation (treble); 299, line 4, answer of the same by contrary motion (bass); 300, line 4 (end), augmentation (tenor); 301, bottom line, an irregular sort of augmentation, combined with close answers in crotchets (bass); 302, line 5, etc., close imitation on second part of the original subject; 303, line 4, eight bar "Pedal" in treble part.

This Fantasia is in the Dorian (transposed) mode, with one flat, showing the changed pitch. It is important to remember that the notion of "key" (in the modern sense) was not invented in the Elizabethan times. It is merely an accident that this piece of Sweelinck's happens to begin with a phrase founded on a chord of D minor, and that the signature seems to correspond. All the flat means here is, that the Dorian mode is moved up a fourth.

Philips' Fantasia (i. 335) is almost equally ingenious in its construction. [Byrd's Fantasia, ii. 406, is on the same subject.]

An interesting feature is (p. 335, l. 3, etc.) the use in episode, of a passage familiar enough one and a half centuries after in Handel's "Amen" Chorus, and in many other 17th and 18th century contrapuntal works.

SPECIMEN OF "HANDELIAN" MATERIAL, FROM THE
16TH CENTURY.

Taken from Fantasia (Fitzwilliam Book, i. 335).

PETER PHILIPS.

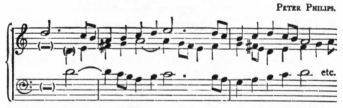

Another curious thing is the fact that the one subject is brought in thirty-nine times (each time carefully numbered). This, there is little doubt, Philips would regard as "an excellent good conceit," referring, in the crooked mystic manner

of the time, to the words of St Paul in 2 Cor. xi. 24, " Of
the Jews five times received I forty stripes save one."
References to contrapuntal subtilties in this piece are:—

> Page 339, l. 3, subject by Augmentation.
>   „ 338, l. 4,   „   Diminution.
>   „ 342, l. 4,   „   Double Diminution.
>   „ 341, l. 4,   „   Close Stretto.

EXTRACT FROM FANTASIA (FITZWILLIAM BOOK, i. 357) BY
NIC. STROGERS (showing system of numbering the
successive appearances of the subject).

N. STROGERS.

The last bars of the same, as beautiful as the former are ugly.

NICHOLAS STROGERS.

Other instructive features of this example of Strogers are —(*a*) The uncompromising nature of the "false relations," *e.g.*, in bars 4 and 8; (*b*) the varying lengths of the "bars," some containing six minims, others four or two, showing that the "signature" refers to the relative lengths of semibreves and minims, not to the size of bars.

CHAPTER VII

FUGAL FANTASIAS (SEVERAL SUBJECTS)

WE now will consider two other Fantasias, in which *several* subjects are used, instead of one only, by Bull (i. 423) and Byrd (i. 188).

In the former (which is in two parts only, except quite at the end), no less than four different subjects appear on p. 423, and several more occur in the following pages. This work of Bull's is, however, very remarkable, on account of the unusual nature of p. 425, where a pedal is introduced, consisting of continual repetition of the following passage in the bass—

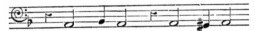

This motive is repeated more than twelve times, and must have been a wonderful, if not alarming, exhibition of continuous purpose to those who first heard it.

Byrd's piece (i. 188) also has several subjects—I., p. 188, ll. 1, 2, 3; II., end of l. 3 to p. 189, l. 3; III., p. 189, l. 3, and onward.

An interesting and very unusual thing is presented at the top of p. 189, viz., a case of literal repetition of a phrase which has already been given at the bottom of the previous page, last bar, etc.

IRREGULAR ANSWERS

We must now pay some attention to the system of Subject and Answer, or *Dux* and *Comes*, as it was often called. As is well known, the method of bringing in the various vocal or instrumental "parts" in a Fugue of the 18th century was cut and dried.   One feature, as students are aware, was, that the voice or part which came second in order of entrance had to imitate the melody enunciated by the first voice or part, but at a different pitch.   To put this commonplace piece of knowledge in a concrete form, supposing the Fugue to be in two "parts," X and Y : X begins, *e.g.*, with a tune made of the first four notes of the major scale of C, viz., c d e f e dd c.

That is the Subject or *Dux*.

Y then joins in and imitates these notes, but instead of beginning on the note C, she begins on the note G, and produces this—g a b c b a a g.   This is the Answer or *Comes*.   In the meantime X proceeds, accompanying the answer with a "Counterpoint" (*i.e.* a melody which fits the answer, but runs "counter" to it, if possible furnishing a contrast of style), for instance :—

Here the lower "part" gives out the subject, beginning in the key of C, on the note C.   The upper part "imitates" this, beginning its "answer" on the note G, and eventually turns the "answer" into the *key* of G, as we call it nowadays.

This method was, as I said, cut and dried in the 18th century, and no one, as a rule, would have dared to vary it.

But this plan was not always so firmly established; and in this connection we will study a few examples, illustrating what may be called the History of Irregular Answers, taking instances which occur in the Fitzwilliam Virginal Book, in Fantasias by Bull and Byrd.

In considering these irregularities (by which word I merely mean cases which do not follow the rule of the 18th century with unanimity), it is well to recollect a trick of G. F. Handel, examples of which may be found in a good many of his fugal oratorio choruses, viz., the method of a "false answer" to the fugue subject. A familiar case is in the "Messiah" (1741), " Blessing and honour " (Worthy is the Lamb). Here the basses (and tenors) give out the subject, " Blessing and honour," in the key of D. It is answered " falsely " by the sopranos, who give out the same notes, still in the key of D. Other cases are easily found in Handel's works, *e.g.*, in " Samson," the final chorus, " Ever to sound His praise," the fugue subject of which has a " false answer " of the same sort. These things are cases of the survival of antique methods in Handel's more modern works.

This irregular method may be seen in the Fantasias of the 16th century, preserved for us in the Fitzwilliam Book. Good specimens are the Fantasias of Bull, i. 423; and of Giles Farnaby, ii. 343.

In the example of Bull the " answer " (p. 423, l. 2) is merely the same notes as the " subject," repeated in a lower octave. This Fantasia has several subjects, *e.g.*, a second and third melody make their appearance on l. 3; both answered regularly. These, however, are succeeded by a fourth subject (end of l. 5), which has a " false " answer, reckoning from the last two crotchets of l. 5. The same thing is observed on p. 424, where the regular " answer " seems almost forgotten.

Giles Farnaby (ii. 343) supplies a like case in his first line.

This is an interesting piece. The subject has been well worn since the 16th century.

Amongst the many who have used it, we remember J. S. Bach, who composes one of the best-known of the forty-eight Preludes and Fugues upon these very notes. Let us not forget that the English Giles Farnaby knew the phrase more than a century before J. S. Bach was heard of. Another point is noticeable at the bottom line of p. 343, bar 2, where a harmony occurs

GILES FARNABY (100 years before Purcell).

which our simple historian gossips have identified with the name of Purcell for so long that it will perhaps never be possible to undo the false impression they have produced, and establish it as dating more than a century earlier. Of course, all who know Tallis's five-part Litany (it is almost universally neglected, by the way) know that this harmony occurs there also, in the setting of " We beseech Thee to *hear* us, good Lord." This takes the passage back still further in point of time, as Tallis was living in the early half of the 16th century.

The first three pages of this Fantasia of Giles Farnaby's are worth playing over. A second subject is introduced on p. 344, l. 3.

EXTRACT FROM GILES FARNABY'S FANTASIA (FITZWILLIAM BOOK, ii. 343) showing "false answer" of the second voice.   Mixolydian Mode.

G. FARNABY (16th Century).

After seventeen more bars like this, a second subject is brought in. A good sample of its working is the following :—

G. FARNABY.

sic

etc.

Byrd's Fantasia (i. 188) in the Æolian Mode is also worth
playing through.   The fact that it has several subjects has
already been mentioned, and that an unusual case of literal
repetition takes place on p. 189, l. 1.   But it is interesting
mainly in that the "answers" are regular.   For instance,
p. 188, top line : four different voices come in, one after the
other, in the order—Tenor, Bass, Alto, Treble.   The first
notes of each, in order, are, E, A, E, A.   This, of course,
is quite "regular," except that the last comer begins at short
notice, only allowing the alto to give out three notes of the
"subject," before chiming in with the "answer."   The next
line again (line 2, bar 1) is nearly regular ; the order, Bass,
Tenor, Treble, (the tenor introduces an imitation of the
subject, beginning on the final crotchet of line 2, continuing
on line 3), Alto (line 3, bar 1) ; first notes (reckoning from
line 2, bar 1, bass), E, A, E (treble last bar, line 2), A (alto,
line 3, bar 1).

A second subject in crotchets begins at the end of line 3
in the alto (the three crotchet *e*'s), answered by the tenor,

and introducing a "tonal" alteration of the "subject," *i.e.*
e e e f is "answered" by a a a c. This may be only
an accident, but it will serve to direct the student's attention
to a new department of the History of Fugues, viz., the
origin of Tonal Fugue as opposed to Real Fugue. (The
latter simply means that the "answer" is a "real" literal
imitation of the "subject," merely altered as to the part of
the scale in which it is written; whereas "Tonal" Fugue
means that the "answer" is altered, more or less, in its
intervals, on account of the thing called "Key," or "Tone.")

Now the fact really is, that the Fantasias of the 16th
century were very generally what *we* call "Real" Fugues.
Those in the Fitzwilliam Book are so, almost without exception. That is to say, the "answers" are literal transcriptions, without alteration (except of pitch) of the "subjects."
This was the case throughout the early history of Fugue.
Now, we must remember always that there were no such
things as "keys" in those days, at least in our modern
sense. The fact that a piece began on the note G, and
ended on a chord of G, did not mean, as it must mean nowadays, that it was in the key of G. The fact that a piece
had a flat in its signature did not mean that it was in the key
of D minor or F major. Such ideas were in their early
infancy in Elizabethan times.

And apparently, it was not until the older methods
associated with "Mode" had been overlaid by the notion of
"Key," that the difficulty of "Tonal" answer in Fugue
made itself felt.

An example will make the meaning of this clear to any
musical person. I take Byrd's Fantasia (i. 37) in the Fitzwilliam Virginal Book. The subject consists of a portion of
the scale of G, including G a b c d. We note, by the
way, that there is no sharp in the signature, although the
piece strikes our modern eye and ear as being in the key

of G major; also it ends on a chord of G; nevertheless, Byrd thought of it as in the Mixolydian Mode, the " final " of which is the note G; and indeed even a beginner will easily notice that the note F is as frequently natural as sharp, and as a fact that the use of the F♯ is much circumscribed throughout.

Now, Byrd makes this a " Real " Fugue, *i.e.* he " answers " the " subject " literally, viz., G a b c d is " answered " by D e f♯ g a, twice in the first two lines. Nevertheless, Byrd felt a difficulty at bar 2, for he wished to bring in the bass at bar 3, and apparently felt that to answer d b G by a f♯ D, would somehow be out of place, and accordingly he alters the answer at bar 2. However, he does not do it again in line 2, so we will let that pass. What it is necessary for us to grasp now is, that the practice of the 18th century (Handel, Bach, etc., etc., etc.) would have been different.

Here is Byrd's practice, and (below) that of the men 150 years later.

FANTASIA in Mixolydian Mode.

W. Byrd (16th Century).

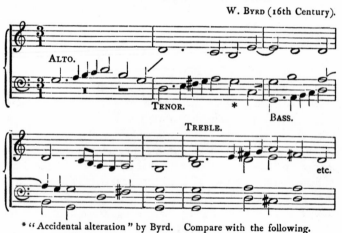

* " Accidental alteration " by Byrd.   Compare with the following.

Fugue on Byrd's subject, as it might have been done by men of the 18th century, who thought in the " key " of G major.

E. W. N.

Byrd's Fugue is Real, the alternative version is " Tonal," *i.e.* the " answer " is *altered* from the " subject " in order to fit with the more modern conception of the " key " of G major, which was not in the mind of William Byrd. In this example of the 18th century method I have taken care not to alter the " style," *e.g.*, the dulness of the alto part, continually returning to the note D, is quite of the 16th century, not of the 18th, which, whatever faults it developed, on the whole avoided dulness in Fugue.

An example of a different kind, which seems to confirm this view, is found in Wasielewski (" Hist. Instr. Mus. XVI. Cent."), who gives an instrumental Fugue (dated 1532) in four

---

* Compare these with the corresponding notes in the *first* bar. The crotchet D is altered, the minim F♯ is not. F♯ is the major third of D, and is the proper tonal answer to the B in bar 1, which is the major third of G.

† These two are the Tonic and Dominant of the scale of G, and are the " regular " answers to the Dominant and Tonic which are observed in bar 1.

parts: where the treble begins the "subject" on C, the alto "answers" it, beginning on F; but the tenor and bass, instead of doing exactly the same over again, and thus preserving the "key effect," go on from the alto with further intervals of a fifth, and begin their repetition of "subject" and "answer" on B♭ and E♭ respectively.

This, of course, has the natural result of lowering the general pitch of the piece by a whole tone at the second appearance of the "answer." The composer seems, however, not to feel the smallest embarrassment in this predicament. Nor is his procedure in any way remarkable, except in that it very naturally fails to exemplify the practice of a *coming* century, which did not draw its life blood either from Modes or Hexachords, but from major and minor scales.

Some few instances from the Fitzwilliam Book will be useful as illustrations of this matter, which is still dealt with in University examinations in Counterpoint.

I will give *five* examples of what appear to be hints of the practice of "Tonal" Fugue in the 16th century. I lay no stress on four of the five, but give them as possible illustrations, no more.

Byrd. Miserere, ii. 232, where, in the first line, A *B♭* is answered in the bass by D *F*, not D *E*.

MISERERE.

W. BYRD (Fitzwilliam Book, ii. 232)

The Alto is the "Canto Fermo."

On p. 233, l. 3, bar 1, there is an obvious mistake in the copy, which causes an *apparent* case of altered "answer"; the alto part should read (in crotchets), A *B* C D, not A C D, and should begin at the fourth beat of the bar, not the fifth.

There is, however, one more genuine alteration of the kind, p. 233, l. 4, last bar and following, where the bass G B C D, etc., is answered by the treble *A* B C D, etc.

But there is reason for not attaching much importance to either of these examples.

Byrd, Fantasia, ii. 408, top line, where C G, in the alto, is answered by G C, in the treble.

But this is apparently set at nought by the "Real" answers which bristle elsewhere in the next two lines, *e.g.*, the *D* G, etc., in the lowest voice of the final bar of the extract given.

Bull, Fantasia on Canto Fermo, i. 138, where in bars 1 and 2, C B A is answered by F E C♯, instead of F E D. Perhaps some little reliance can be placed on this, as the Canto Fermo does not make it *impossible* for the answer to be "Real"; in fact it would go better and more pleasantly thus :—

etc.

Compare bars 2 and 3 (treble) of this alteration with the original.

FANTASIA ON CANTO FERMO

JOHN BULL (Fitzwilliam Book, i. 138).

etc.

It is quite clear that the alteration, with " Real " answer, makes the passage more easy and natural. Therefore it seems possible that here Bull really had some slight intention of giving the subject a " Tonal " answer, even at the cost of graceful melody or pleasing harmony.

Morley, ii. 57, gives what is apparently a " Tonal " reply on line 1, A to E being answered by E to A. This is a trivial instance.

The *only case*, however, which appears really certain, and to be mentioned with confidence, is

Byrd, Fantasia, i. 406, where the (comparatively) unimportant scale of eight notes from C is answered by a corresponding scale of eight notes from G; but in the subsequent crotchets which complete the subject, the notes C *A* B G, etc., are answered by G *D* E C, etc., thus bringing the music back into the right key.

FANTASIA.

W. Byrd (Fitzwilliam Book, i. 406).

Also see the last three bars, on p. 410, where the treble *C E* F G is answered in the alto by *G A* B C.

William Byrd.

End of the same piece.

An apparently plain case of a plagal answer to a Fugue, is that of Thomas Tallis, "Felix Namque" (No. 2), on page 1 of volume ii., and dated 1564.

The first four and a half lines of this work are a fugal exposition of a subject, three semibreves in length, where the main notes, A D, are answered by D A, with almost perfect consistency. The one irregularity is in the treble, l. 2, bar 1, where the A is reached from E instead of D. This is a good example, as the subject or the answer appears no less than seven times in the four and a half lines.

A difficulty in reconciling the practice of Tallis in this piece with the Modal Theory seems to be, that as the work is in the Æolian Mode, the plagal answer to the note A would be E, not D. It is sufficient to say here that the answer is unusual, and doubtless to be regarded as an effort towards the creation of a new " phase " of the mode.

CHAPTER VIII

SONGS OF THE 16TH CENTURY

OF popular songs, Shakespearian and otherwise, a large number are given in the Fitzwilliam Book. As with the dance tunes, so with the songs; they are used for the production of variations, mostly of the kind already familiar to those who have studied the dances of the Fitzwilliam Book, *i.e.* the variations are merely ornamental, consisting of running passages and florid semi-contrapuntal overlayings of the tune. This as a general rule; there are a few cases where the possibility of other methods seems to have been felt, *e.g.*, Giles Farnaby's " Daphne " (ii. 12):—

FIRST PHRASE OF THE FIRST STRAIN OF " DAPHNE," SET
  BY GILES FARNABY (FITZWILLIAM BOOK, ii. 12). For
  the words, see Chappell, i. 150 (Wooldridge ed.).

The " Rep." or Variation on the same.

Last phrase of the third strain of "Daphne."

Varied thus on p. 14, with the melody in the left hand part :—

etc.

where on p. 14, line 5, the melody is in the tenor, and the right hand has a florid passage, indicating the harmony very clearly, and going in a contrary direction to the melody. Again, William Byrd's " Walsingham," i. 267 (a much more artistic work than Bull's on the same tune, i. 1), where variations 2, 3, 4, treat the melody by imitation, instead of mere *agrémens* or ornamentation ; also variation 5 (pp. 267-68), where the melody is in the bass, and the other voices have imitations founded on the melody itself.

VARIATION 5 ON " WALSINGHAM " (with the tune in the Bass, and accompanied by imitations). See below, p. 119, for the plain melody.

BYRD (1538-1623).

(a) In bar 2, the low D is omitted by Byrd, as it is out of reach.

(b) In bar 4, the bass is ingeniously made to answer an imitation leading to the coming phrase of the melody at bar 5.

(c) The melody relapses into the conventional bass of a cadence at the third crotchet of bar 7.

(d) Observe the time signature, which neither prescribes nor disallows triple rhythm.

This work of Byrd's is of great interest and value, and shows Byrd at his best, which means a good deal. Other interesting passages are, variations 13 (tune nearly always *inside* the chords), 14 (curiously like a well-known passage in Wagner's "Siegfried Idyll," or would be, if the tune was played on an oboe, and the left-hand part *legato* on strings),

ANTICIPATION OF WAGNER'S "SIEGFRIED IDYLL" IN BYRD'S
   "WALSINGHAM" VARIATIONS (FITZWILLIAM VIRGINAL
   BOOK, i. 270).

BYRD (1538-1623).

Variation 14.

16 (not unmusical in its use of the rhythm of 3 against 2, whereas Bull's exploits in this line are often merely clever and ugly), and 22 (where at page 273, line 3, bar 2, the melody is missing in the copy, b c d, being two crotchets and a minim). Still again, the anonymous setting of "Barafostus' Dreame," i. 72 (? whether Dreame = Dreme, *i.e.* "Song," for the only words that seem to be known to it are those in Chappell's "Old English Popular Music," vol. i. 148, called "The Shepherd's Joy"). In this work the third variation (last line of p. 72) hides the tune in the tenor, and introduces above it a sort of canon in quavers between treble and alto.

First Line of "Barafostus' Dreame" (set by an anonymous composer of the 16th century, who may be William Byrd, judging by the style).

THE 3RD VARIATION ON THE ABOVE (showing the tune in the tenor, accompanied by a well-marked "figure" in imitation).

(*a*) In line 1, bar 3 (containing three dotted minims, in contrast to the bars preceding and following), two crotchet rests appear wanting in the R. H.

(*b*) In line 2, the treble resumes the melody in bar 3 at the f♮.

(*c*) There is probably some correction to be made in the last bar given above, marked (?). Most likely the first quaver R. H. ought to be "f," not "g."

(d) These extracts contain two instances of a sign or obliteration of a sign which has puzzled students of the MS., viz., (applied to the crotchet " g " in the R. H. of bar 3 of the former line, and (occurs with quaver " b flat " in the last bar R. H. of the latter specimen). Nothing seems known of them, if they really are ornaments. Probably they are merely obliterations of the single and double line, explained above, p. 32.

However, on the whole, the variations on these songs are not of any greater interest than those we have already considered in connection with Pavans and Galliards, etc.

The real interest of these songs is that they must have been *popular*, since so many variations were written on them. Besides this testimony, the allusions to many of them in contemporary plays are numerous, and we remember that a song would have to be a household word with the public before it rose to be mentioned familiarly on the stage.

Some of them are actually songs used in plays of Shakespeare, *e.g.*, " O mistress mine " ; more commonly, however, they are alluded to, or quoted, *e.g.*, Callino Casturame, Walsingham, Fortune, Robin.

The total number of songs in the Fitzwilliam Book is about forty-two. The number is slightly doubtful, because one or two are not *certainly* songs, for no words seem to be known, nor any connection with words ; *e.g.*, " Heaven and Earth " (i. 415), by F. Tregian, which is almost surely an ecclesiastical piece, and not a song.

Six of the forty-two songs have two arrangements, this, I suppose, tending to show that they were even more popular than the others. Such are, " Go from my window " (Morley, i. 42, and Munday, i. 153 ; but these are nearly the same, and probably the double ascription is a blunder), " The woods so wilde" (Byrd, i. 263, and Gibbons, i. 144), "Walsing-ham" (Bull, i. 1, and Byrd, i. 267), "Why aske you" (*Anon.*, ii. 192, and G. Farnaby, ii. 462), "Barafostus' Dream" (*Anon.*, i. 72, and T. Tomkins, ii. 94), and "Bonny Sweet Robin" (G. Farnaby, ii. 77, and J. Munday, i. 66).

We will make a beginning with five songs from the Fitz-william Book which are used or alluded to in Shakespeare. (I omit "Hanskin," ii. 494, which *may* belong to "Jog on," Autolycus' song in "A Winter's Tale.")

The very first piece in the Fitzwilliam Book is the varia-tions by Bull on "Walsingham." "Walsingham" is an ancient tune, probably belonging to the quite early 16th century,* and is associated with various sets of words dealing with the visits of pilgrims to the shrine of Our Lady of Walsingham in Norfolk. This shrine was cele-brated in the time of Henry III. (who was there in 1241), of Edward I. (who visited it in 1280 and 1296), and of Edward II. (in 1315). Henry VII. spent Christmas of 1486-87 at Norwich, and made a pilgrimage from there to Walsingham; and next summer, after the battle of Stoke, he sent his banner to be offered before Our Lady of Walsingham.

It was said that the Milky Way pointed directly to the home of the Virgin, to guide pilgrims on their road; hence it was called the "Walsingham Way." Also crosses at every town pointed the way to Walsingham along the earthly counterpart of this heavenly path.

Catherine of Arragon, when dying, recommended her soul to Our Lady at Walsingham; and so did her royal husband. Thus the reputation of the place was very great at the beginning of the 16th century, and had been so for 300 years. But this came to an end in 1538, when

* For the plain melody of "Walsingham," see below, p. 119.

the priory was dissolved, the image of Our Lady being burned at Chelsea by the commissioners ; and the gains of the Norfolk people were stopped at their source.

The Percy Folio Manuscript (ed. Hales and Furnivall, Trübner, 1868), vol. iii. p. 471, gives the words of an ancient ballad which goes to the tune as it is in the Fitzwilliam Book, and contains a line or two of Ophelia's scattered scraps of songs in "Hamlet," *e.g.*, "How shold I know your true loue | that haue met many a one," etc.

Dent's "Shakespeare's Songs" gives the three verses (p. 77) sung by Ophelia in "Hamlet," iv. 5, which are part of an old ballad on similar lines to that in the Percy Folio.

Caulfield's "Collection of Shakespeare Vocal Music" (1864) gives the tunes and portions of tunes to which actresses traditionally sang Ophelia's quotations. These are printed in "Shakespeare and Music" (Dent, 1896), p. 196, where the traditional air for "How should I your true love know ?" etc., is clearly a corrupt form of the tune "Walsingham" in the Fitzwilliam Book.

Percy's Reliques (Bohn, vol. i. p. 312) gives a single verse, quoted from the Pepysian collection, which also goes to this tune.

The old ballad from the Percy Folio is a dialogue between a lover who has lost his love, and a pilgrim whom he meets returning from Walsingham, which was known as the English "Holy Land."

I venture to suggest that Byrd had this dialogue form in his mind, when he set his first harmony of "Walsingham," as it may be seen in the Fitzwilliam Book (i. 267), obviously portraying two persons singing alternate lines of the poem.

Callino Casturame (corruption of Irish, "Colleen oge Asthore"). It has already been mentioned that Shakespeare's Pistol refers to this song in "Henry V." iv. 4,

l. 4. It is a charming tune, and the words may be seen in Chappell, i. 84. The words of the title are used as a refrain, so the tune has to be sung nine times to get through the verses.

The words as given there were printed in 1584.

"*Fortune my Foe*," or "Fortune." This tune is set by Byrd (i. 254). One verse is given in Chappell (i. 76), but only for want of anything older, for it is probably not the original set of words. Shakespeare mentions the tune in "Merry Wives," iii. 3, l. 62 :—

Falstaff [to Mrs Ford]. I see what thou wert, if Fortune thy Foe were not, Nature thy friend.

A number of songs were sung to this tune, and in the 17th century it was used largely for doleful and lugubrious verses. Thus in 1634 it was spoken of as "the hanging tune," and in 1641, "that preaching tune," in connection with songs concerning the execution of criminals.

A much earlier instance of this is dated 1588-89, "The judgment of God shewed upon Dr John Faustus : tune, Fortune my Foe." This has woodcuts of Dr Faustus signing the contract with the devil, etc.

Moreover, the old ballad of "Titus Andronicus," on which the so-called Shakespeare play was founded, was also sung to "Fortune," and with propriety, judging by this rule, for nothing could be more gloomy than the story (Percy Reliques, Bohn, vol. i. p. 162), or more dreary, for there are thirty verses of it.

Robin, or "*Bonny Sweet Robin*," set by Giles Farnaby (ii. 77); and John Munday (i. 66). Farnaby's the longest and best. The tune is in "Shakespeare and Music," p. 198.

Scarcely any words remain, but the one line sung by Ophelia in Hamlet, "For bonny sweet Robin is all my joy," and a line which may or may not have some connection with it, "My Robin is to the greenwood gone,"

For the sake of having some words, I have strung together two verses, including these two lines, which can be used for this tune: —

> " My Robin is to the greenwood gone,
> My Robin has left me quite alone.
> Sad are the days, alas,
> Slowly the hours do pass :
> Bonny sweet Robin is all my moan.
>
> My heart is sore with all annoy,
> My thoughts are set in one employ.
> Weeping I grieve for him,
> All would I leave for him :
> Bonny sweet Robin is all my joy."

" *O Mistress mine.*" This, of course, is a complete Shakespeare song, " Twelfth Night," ii. 3. The clown sings it to Sir Andrew and Sir Toby.

The tune is set by Byrd (i. 258), and there are six variations, well worth hearing. It was also set by Morley, but this version is not in the Fitzwilliam Book.

Of those songs which are not Shakespearian, one of the best is "*Barafostus' Dream*," already mentioned. It is set by Tomkins (ii. 94), whose work is difficult to play; also by an anonymous writer (i. 72), whose composition is more valuable artistically, though much shorter. I suspect it may be Byrd's, on account of the general style, which is more concerned with the display of the possibilities in the given melody, than with the display of the virtuosity of the performer ; also on account of vars. 3 and 4, which tend to " disguise" the tune rather than to over-ornament it. (See above, pp. 83, 84.)

Chappell (i. 148) gives a set of words called " The Shepherd's Joy."

Another beautiful tune is *Daphne* (see above, p. 79), set by

Giles Farnaby (ii. 12).   The melody has three strains, and a variation on each strain is introduced before the next is played.   Interesting passages are: p. 14, l. 5, where the tune is in the *left* hand; and p. 15, l. 5, where the rhythm of three against two occurs in the bass staff, accompanied by a passage in broken thirds, which is really an ornament of the plain harmony set to the last two bars of sect. 1 or sect. 3.

Chappell (i. 150) gives two pleasant verses.

A good example of the humorous song of the 16th century is *Martin said to his Man.*

This is set (ii. 275) by *Anon.* with one variation only, and the words are supplied by Chappell (i. 140), who says they were printed in 1588.

Under this heading may also be included *Go from my window* (i. 42 or i. 153, either by Morley or Munday), some words of which are in Chappell (i. 146, 147); and *John, come kiss me now,* set by Byrd (i. 47), one verse being in Chappell (i. 269).   Various other verses are preserved in MS. in the library of Trinity College, Dublin.

These were printed in "Longman's Magazine," vol. xxvii., November 1895, and are here given, with the tune, from the Fitzwilliam Virginal Book.

"JHON COME KISSE ME NOW."

Harmony imitated from WILLIAM BYRD, in Fitzwilliam Book, i. 47, by E. W. N.

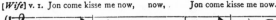

[*Wife*] v. 1. Jon come kisse me now, now,   Jon come kisse me now.

Jon come kisse me by-and-by, and mak no mor a - dow.

This is followed by *His answer to yt sam toone.*

[*Husband*]

v. 2. Peace I'm angrie now, now, peace I'm angrie now,
Peace I'm angrie at the hert, and knowe not qt to dow.

Here is an example of the way this tune may be fitted to the next eleven verses.

Husband]

v. 3. Wyfs can faine and wyfs can flatter: heav I not hit them now: When

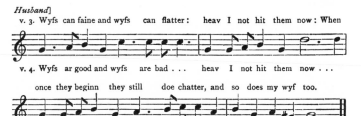

v. 4. Wyfs ar good and wyfs are bad ... heav I not hit them now ...

once they beginn they still doe chatter, and so does my wyf too.

Wyfs... can make ther hus - bands mad: and so does my wyf too.

The rest of the song (verses 5-14) is as follows :—

5. Wyfs can sport and wyfs can play : heav I not, etc.
And wt little work passe ower the day, and so does, etc.

6. And wyfs hes many fair words and looks : heav I not, etc.
And draws sillie men on folies hooks : and so did my wyf too.

7. Wyfs will not ther meetting misse : heav I not, etc.
A cowp of seck they can well kisse : and so can, etc.

8. Wyfs can dance and wyfs can lowp : heav I not, etc.
   Wyfs can toome the full wyne stowp : and so can, etc.

9. Wyfs can ban and wyfs can curse : heav I not, etc.
   Wyfs can toome ther husband's purse ; and so can, etc.

10. Wyfs can flyte and wyfs can scold : heav I not, etc.
    Wyfs of ther toungs they heav no hold : and nane hes
    my wyf too.

11. Wyfs they'r good then at no tym, neither is my wyf now,
    Except it be in drinking wyn, and so is my wyf too.

12. Some they be right needful evills, so is my wyf now,
    Wyfs ar nothing else but divles, and so is my wyf too.

13. Now of my song I make ane end, lo heir I quyt the now,
    All evill wyfs to the divle I send, amongst them my
    wyf too.

14. Peace I'm angrie now, now, peace I'm angrie now,
    Peace I'm angrie at the hert and cannot tell qt to dowe.

One more good tune is *Rowland*, set by Byrd (ii. 190) :—

" ROWLAND," OMITTING " REP."

(FITZWILLIAM BOOK, ii. 190).

W. BYRD (1358-1623).

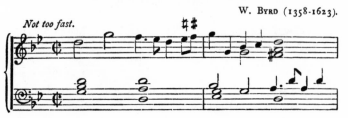

Chappell gives two verses of the song " Lord Willoughby's March," as belonging to this tune, but they fit badly enough.

"*The woods so wilde*," or " As I walked the wood so wild," is set by Byrd (i. 263) and Gibbons (i. 144). A short extract is given below, see p. 145.

The words are not extant, but the poetry of the subject was plainly realised in the setting of Byrd, who shows unmistakable signs of picturing the rustle of the great forest, and the woodland atmosphere generally. Orlando Gibbons' setting is more wooden; still there is something poetical about it, as one would expect from him, and as is *not* to be expected from Bull.

CHAPTER IX

" FANCY " PIECES

A SMALL but remarkable class of works in the Fitzwilliam Virginal Book is that of " Fancy Pieces."

Some of these are, Byrd's " The Bells " (i. 274), John Munday's Fantasia on the Weather (i. 23), and Giles Farnaby's three pieces (ii. 260-62), called—

(1) " Giles Farnaby's Dream " (a Pavana).

(2) " His Rest " (a Galliard).

(3) " His Humour."

GILES FARNABY'S DREAME (FITZWILLIAM

BOOK, ii. 260).

G. FARNABY (16th Century).

The mordents marked in the MS. (only two) are given. For other examples of the final repetition of the chord of the key, see above, p. 32, and below, p. 132.

There is also a piece by Munday (ii. 449) called " Munday's Joy," but it is of no special interest except in the form of the title, and may be classed with (ii. 257) " Doctor Bull's my selfe," a Gigge, which consists of a couple of ordinary

variations on a rather comical $\frac{6}{4}$ tune, otherwise not remarkable.

Another little piece is " Farnabye's Conceit " (ii. 424), not
very remarkable.

Munday's " Fantasia on the Weather," though interesting,
is mere experiment when compared with Byrd's " Bells."

The various meteorological events, Faire Wether, Lightning, Thunder, Calme Wether, Lightning, Thunder, Faire
Wether, Lightning, Thunder, Faire Wether, Lightning,
Thunder, and finally " A CLEARE DAY," are successively
imitated by Mr J. Munday ; and the piece is about as truly
affecting as the simple list of phenomena named above. (The
very first note of this piece probably ought to be A, not G.
Also the note C♯ in line 3, queried by the editors, may well
be right.)

I class it with the " Battle of Prague," a very popular
after-dinner piece about 1830, containing indications (in print)
of the passages which were supposed to represent the advance
of cavalry, the rattle of musketry fire, the groans of the
wounded, and the other noises of war ; the whole con-
cluding with " Malbrouk " and " God save the King," as in
duty bound.

Before leaving this, we may remind ourselves that Munday's
attempt is a very early specimen of " programme music," and
thus is worth looking at, in spite of its comparatively small
musical value, as representing the 16th century. Later
composers whose names are associated with the growth of
programme music, are Kuhnau (lived late in the 17th century),
whose " Biblical Sonatas " (pub. 1700), aiming at the representation of well-known scriptural stories, are interesting
both as music and as exemplifying a stage in the history of
descriptive music (a modern reprint is to be had), and J. S.
Bach, who in the early part of the 18th century wrote his
" Capriccio on the Departure of a Friend," representing the

farewell speeches of acquaintances, the laments and tears of friends, their final leave-taking, the arrival of the coach, and the journey, enlivened by an active posthorn.

Later still, we have Beethoven's Sonata in E♭, representing not only the departure, but the absence and return of a friend.

Thus John Munday's 16th century piece deserves more than passing mention, although there were others of about his time, *e.g.*, Frohberger (d. 1667), who tried their hands at programme music with such success as was possible.

But Byrd's "Bells" (i. 274) is in every way more valuable. This piece convinces me that Byrd was more of a musician than Bull. It is a genuine attempt to embody the *romance* of church bells, in terms of the art of the 16th century, and without any of the vanity of technique which stares one in the face in almost all Bull's compositions. Points of interest in this piece are :—

(1) P. 274, line 1, the bells "ring up," beginning with the "tenor" (or largest bell). This is still the practice of change ringers.

(2) Throughout the whole piece Byrd never fails to remember that the lowest bells, especially the "tenor," are the most impressive. This is common knowledge to persons who have often listened to "changes," especially on large peals of ten or twelve bells. It is even the case that the three or four lowest bells in such a peal are the only ones to pierce through the general jangle, and preserve their separate existence. This is very apparent at a considerable distance. Byrd attempts, with some success, to realise this general effect.

(3) An example of the effect of wind or atmospheric change, such as is commonly noticed. It is indicated, not by *f* and *p*, for the virginals could not achieve this, but by a difference in the octave. See ll. 3 to 6.

(4) P. 279, var. 9, where the gradual weakening of the " peal," produced by " ringing down," is depicted. This is especially clear in the last line but one, where the little incomplete descending scales, tumbling over one another, are quite characteristic of the effect referred to.

" The Bells " may well be associated with " The woods so wilde" (i. 263) of the same composer (dated 1590), or " Walsingham " (i. 267) in this respect. All three pieces stamp Byrd as a " romantic." For a contrast with Bull, the settings of " Walsingham " may be directly compared, as both writers have dealt with this melody (Bull's, i. 1).

All three of these compositions of Byrd are worth hearing, and deserve any pains to bring out the expressive power that they certainly possess.

The " Romantic" quality of Byrd is well shown in his " Cantiones Sacræ " (some of which are still sung in Cathedral services as anthems)—better shown in these than in the virginal music, inasmuch as the voice was a perfect instrument even in the 16th century, whereas the virginals were far below the pianoforte, even below a bad pianoforte. One must remember (it is easy to forget) that the virginals (also the similar ordinary harpsichord of a later time) had no expressive power whatever, no possibility of soft and loud, or mechanism which would allow of different vocal " parts " being made prominent or the reverse. Consequently the virginal music does not do the same *justice* to its composer as the vocal compositions do.

Giles Farnaby's three little "fancy" pieces are all very short, but undoubtedly are what is now called " characteristic."

(1) Giles Farnaby's " Dreame " (ii. 260) is clearly a poetical effort, and contains three sections, all of a placid character. " Formally," *i.e.* in respect of its time and number of strains, it is a Pavan ; but its " character " is certainly not that of the usual square cut dance.

(2) " His Rest." This, in form, is a Galliard, *i.e.* it has three strains and is in triple time, but the title is easily justified by sympathetic playing.

(3) " His Humour," on the next page, is only longer than the two former pieces, because variations (called " Rep.") are added to some of the phrases.

The word "humour" in Shakespeare (which should give us Giles Farnaby's general understanding of the word) indicates a "wayward" fancy.

Hence this piece is named. It is not Pavan, Galliard, Fantasia (or Fugue), Alman, Gigge, Air, or what not; it is "His Humour," or wayward fancy. The "Humour" is plain, and is seen in the chromaticism of line 2, and the sudden slow pace of the minims, after the crotchets and quavers of line 1, and in the mild joke of setting the Hexachord in section 4.

CHAPTER X

HEXACHORDS

THIS brings us to a very remarkable class of six works on the Hexachord,* or

Ut, Re, Mi, Fa, Sol, La.

One is by Sweelinck (ii. 26), two by Byrd (i. 395; i. 401, Ut, mi, re, fa, etc.); two by Bull (i. 183; ii. 281), and the passage of Farnaby already named (ii. 262).

* The word Hexachord means "six notes," and is the ancient (11th century) name for the three scales which the mediæval writers referred to in their "Gamut." It is easily understood by an illustration—

    I.   II.   III.

ut re mi fa sol la | ut re mi fa sol la | ut re mi fa sol la

I. is the *Hexachoraum Durum*.

II. is *Hexachordum Naturale*.

III. is *Hexachordum Molle*, or "soft" Hexachord, the word "soft" referring to the Bémol, or B *flat*.

It will be observed that these scales of six notes are all exactly similar in respect of their tones and semitones, viz., they are the same as the first six notes of our modern Major Scale.

The first G, a later addition (for obviously the original scale must have been named from A), was known as Gam-Ut, being marked by the Greek letter gamma, whereas the other two Ut's were C fa ut, and F fa ut, the double "solfa" names having the effect of deciding the actual octave in which the note referred to was to be found. "Tenor" C, for instance, is *Fa* in Hexachord I, and *Ut* in Hexachord II, thus it was known as C fa ut. A more complicated case would be the C above, viz., "middle" C, which would be called C sol fa ut, a compound of the names of C in all three Hexachords.

These pieces introduce us to a subject which is as difficult as it is interesting to the student of musical history, namely, the origin of "Key" in the modern sense. In close attendance on this, there is also presented the question of the History of Temperament (*i.e.* the question of how musical instruments should be "tuned"), which has always been a trouble to the practical musician, and probably always will be, in spite of the labours of such enthusiasts as Perronet-Thompson and other acousticians of the 19th century.

In the first place, these pieces are a living demonstration of the fact that the Hexachord was the only notion of a scale, in *our* sense, that the classic 16th century possessed.

This is important, as it shows us one reason why the notion of "Key" was so slow in coming to the front. What I mean is, that the Hexachord could not "define" a "Key" so completely as our more recent scales do, inasmuch as it was without a "Leading" Note, *i.e.* the top note but one, which we regard as a strong characteristic of any key, major or minor.

Secondly, Bull's work on this subject (i. 183) introduces in a remarkably bold manner the question of Temperament,*

* A most valuable experiment may be made by any student who wishes to have a clear notion of "Temperament," and the physical limits of Harmony. All that is necessary can be done on a small harmonium with one set of reeds, or on one set of pipes in a church organ. The method of tuning the small number of twelve semitones in the octave, which such an instrument presents, so as to give "just" intonation, as far as those twelve sounds can do it, is described in the following diagram given to me by Mr G. T. Bennett of Emmanuel College, who has himself tuned, or mis-tuned, a harmonium in the Cavendish Laboratory in this very way :—

$$\begin{array}{llll} \text{A} & \text{E} & \text{B} & \text{F}\sharp \\ \text{F} & \text{C} & \text{G} & \text{D} \\ \text{D}\flat & \text{A}\flat & \text{E}\flat & \text{B}\flat \end{array}$$

This scheme, read *horizontally*, gives a series of perfect 5ths which are to be tuned exactly "just," *i.e.* as a violinist tunes his 5ths, in perfect "intonation," so that there are *no* beats, and the vibration numbers of the two notes and shows plainly that the difficulties of "Enharmonic" change of key had presented themselves very completely to the musicians of the Tudor period, long before John Jenkins wrote his Fancy for three viols (1667 (see the MS. at York) which modulates through flat keys from F to (nearly) D flat ; and longer still before J. S. Bach wrote the 48 Preludes and Fugues in *every key* for which a name existed.

bear the precise relation of $\frac{3}{2}$—*e.g.*, in the top line, A E, E B, B F♯, where the second note of each pair is the higher in pitch.

Read *vertically*, the scheme shows "just" major 3rds, which are to be tuned similarly until no beats are perceived, exactly in the proportion $\frac{5}{4}$, *e.g.*, in the fourth column, F♯ D, D B♭, where the second note of each pair is the lower in pitch.

Proceed in this way until the "octave" is "set," and the medium portion of the keyboard is tuned "just"; then try simple chords of three notes in close harmony.

It is no exaggeration to say that the unaccustomed observer will find himself provided with a new sensation in every combination which he cares to test. The perfect musical beauty of a few (a very few), and the dreadful cacophony of most harmonies which can be produced in this way, is quite beyond description. Here is Nature's final word to the artist in sounds, an "everlasting No." In practical music, perfect intonation *cannot be*, except occasionally, and more or less by accident, in the case of voices and certain orchestral instruments. In the case of pianoforte and organ, from 72 to 100 separate sounds in each octave would be required to ensure the result. This clearly cannot be thought of except as a scientific toy. Compromise is the only resource; either "mean-tone" temperament (where certain chords are better than others, and some are impossible) or "equal" temperament (where all chords are possible, and none are perfect).

The following particulars as to the major and minor common chords on the harmonium tuned as described above, will be of interest: (*a*) C G F have both major and minor triads *good;* (*b*) D F♯ B♭ have both major and minor triads *bad;* (*c*) D♭ E♭ A♭ have major *good*, minor *bad;* and (*d*) E A B have major *bad*, minor *good*. Thus 12 out of 24 common chords are unusable ; and chords of greater complexity than these are naturally worse still, as a rule. This series of chords sounds beautifully smooth,

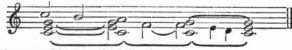

but if transposed into A major it is unbearable.

In a sense, Bull's piece recognises the question more completely than Bach's work, inasmuch as he tries to use the idea of "enharmonics" to produce "modulation" (*i.e.* a *change* of "key"), which was only in a limited sense the object of Bach.

Bull's work is not alone here, for Byrd's composition (i. 395) bears evident marks * of a leaning towards a practical adoption of some scheme of "temperament" which should make a free "modulation" possible—such a modulation as he, above all others of his time, was capable of *imagining*, if not of completely realising.

Byrd's "Ut, Mi, Re" (i. 401) also has hints of a "key" of D major.

William Tisdall's "Pavana Chromatica" (ii. 278) (Mrs Katherin Tregian's Paven) is to be considered another piece of evidence, so much of it being in a "key" requiring five sharps. This is not a mere literal "transposing" (in our modern sense) of a "Mode," for the 2nd strain (p. 279) is frankly Mixolydian, and only has one accidental sharp, viz., F♯, as is so common in that Mode.

Bull's experiment (i. 183) follows the plan of giving the Hexachord (harmonised), beginning first on G (the ancient *Hexachordum Durum* of the 11th century), and then on A, B, etc., a tone higher each time, regardless of consequences. Almost at once he is confronted by heavy troubles. G A B C D E is all very well; A B C♯ D E F♯ is

---

* *E.g.*, i. 397, l. 4, where the chord of A flat major occurs. This was unbearably out of tune on the old "unequal" (mean-tone) temperament, which was still in use in English church organs last century, even in the memory of many persons now living. Also, p. 398, last line, where the chord of E major is used. This also was painfully bad on the "unequal" temperament. Therefore it seems more than likely that both Bull and Byrd used a modified form of tuning, closely resembling the "equal" temperament now universally adopted for all our keyed instruments, *e.g.*, pianofortes and harmoniums.

not very unfamiliar to the Elizabethan mind, but B C♯ D♯ E
F♯ G♯ is decidedly eccentric; while the next repetition (No.
4), beginning on C♯, puzzles the composer with its necessary
sharp to every one of the six notes. Wherefore he tries
changing the *names* of the notes (in practical music that is
really all that is meant by "enharmonic" change), and calls
the 4th repetition D♭ E♭ F G♭ A♭ B♭. Here, one would say,
Bull was little better off, for the number of flats is all but as
great as the number of sharps would have been. But, owing
to the nature of the mediæval system of music, flats were
more familiar to composers, *e.g.*, the system of Modal Transposition even resulted in a *signature* of as many as two flats,
apart from "accidentals."

But at this point Bull finds another difficulty; on the very
chord marked by the 4 indicating the beginning of the 4th
Hexachord, he is brought up with a round turn by the
necessary names of the notes in the "common" chord, which,
with the D♭ above mentioned, completes the harmony of the
moment. These should have been, according to our more
modern practice, bass and tenor (same note), B double flat,
treble F flat. One can imagine Bull thinking over this little
problem in notation. "Who" (he might say), "who ever
heard of such a thing as F flat or B double flat? They
will say John Bull is mad. Call them E and A respectively."

Having repeated the Hexachord six times, rising a *whole
tone* each time, Bull finds his rope has no loose end, but leads
back to his starting-point, so he makes a dive from F to
A♭ (in the bass this time, p. 184, line 5), whence he starts
a new series of repetitions from A♭, B♭, C, D, E. Having
got to E, he is involved in a maze of sharps, as formerly of
flats, and cuts the knot, after putting in F♯ G♯ A♯ B C♯ D♯,
by slipping from the F♯ to G♮, and so preparing the way for
home at var. 14, which, with 15, 16, and 17, are all har-
monisations of the Hexachord on G, and finish the work.

The example by Byrd, however (i. 395), is at once less complete and more musical than the experiment of Bull. In fact, Byrd's setting of the Hexachord is much more truly described as a "Fantasia" (Fugue) on the "subject" G A B C D E. This is well enough shown on the very first page, both in the "answers" of various "parts" and in the use of the "subject" in different forms, while the *notes* of the hexachord are preserved, but not necessarily in the same *lengths* or the same rhythmical formula. Another feature is (*e.g.*, p. 397, lines 1, 2, 3) where the hexachord is accompanied by "imitations," in the other "parts," of a secondary "subject," in crotchets, dotted crotchets, and quavers.

Similar remarks are to be made on Byrd's other composition on this subject (p. 401), where the *order* of the notes in the hexachord is changed, *i.e.* instead of G *A B C D* E, the order is G *B A C B D C* E, thus introducing a new source of variety in the setting. Here again we see the essential difference between Byrd and Bull.

Bull's mind was logical and complete in its own circle, not liable to be turned aside by any considerations of traditional beauty. Indeed, in the piece considered above, he shows himself a ruthless artist, and for that reason I can hardly take the result too seriously as a contribution to the New Music that was surely passing its obscure infancy in the England of Elizabeth, James, and Charles.

Still, we must take what is offered, and make what can be made of it, without going too far in an over-estimate of its value as evidence. Page 183, line 5, contains a convincing transition from what we must call the "Key of E major" to that of D flat.

This is startling, but the effect is more than fairly smooth and reasonable.

JOHN BULL. (1563-1628).

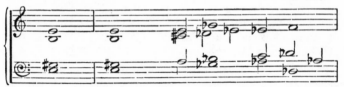

The figure 4 marks the beginning of a Hexachord (the fourth repetition) on D♭ in the alto (here altered for clearness of reading to C♯ *tied* to D♭).

The chords are more easily appreciated as a modulation in this simplified form :—

The same, simplified.

Page 184, l. 5, presents us with a sudden, but by no means harsh modulation, from the harmony of " F major " to " D flat," which is perfectly satisfactory to the ear.

JOHN BULL.

If these instances seem trivial to any student, he may take it as a proof that he is sufficiently corrupted by the music of the 19th century, and that he should by all means take a course of Italian 16th century madrigals or masses, to convince him of his highly coloured misunderstanding. In his present state he is incapable of dealing with the subject, whether he wishes or no.

But this matter of "modulation" (in our modern sense) must be left for discussion elsewhere.

The work of J. P. Sweelinck on "Ut, Re, Mi, Fa, Sol, La" (ii. 26) is a very good piece, and worth playing. It is not only an exercise on the Hexachord, but (as with Byrd's, see above) is a regular fugal "Fantasia" or "Fancy," with independent subjects which maintain their existence, along with and in conjunction with the Hexachord. The first two lines are enough to show this clearly—

"Ut, Re, Mi, Fa, Sol, La," a 4 voci,

Dated 1612.

J. P. SWEELINCK.

where the tenor and treble start a "subject" in a fugal manner, and the bass joins in at bar 3 with the Hexachord F G A B♭ C D,* proceeding then in the next bar to "answer" the subject already given out twice.

* F G A B♭ C D was the "Hexachordum Molle" of the 11th century, so called because of the B♭, or Bémol, "softened B."

An excellent specimen of the cleverness of contrapuntal device, combined with good musical effect, which was attained by the *best* 16th century writers, is the passage on p. 27, line 5, where the alto, tenor, and bass have the "subject" given above, in very close "stretto" (*i.e.* "answered" as close together as possible), and at the same time in "contrary motion," accompanied simultaneously by the Hexachord (descending) in the treble.

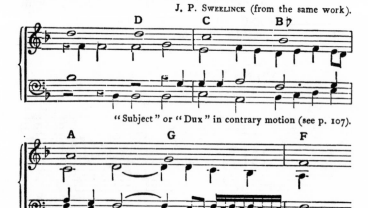

J. P. SWEELINCK (from the same work).

"Subject" or "Dux" in contrary motion (see p. 107).

Once again it is found interesting and curious to notice how very old is the "material" of G. F. Handel (150 years later than Sweelinck), and to compare Handel's "He led them," "as through a wilderness" (Israel in Egypt, No. 13), with the Fitzwilliam Virginal Book, ii. 31, line 2, and following lines.

The "Coda" on p. 33 is worth attention, presenting the Hexachord in close imitation, in quavers and crotchets, instead of semibreves, and accompanied by a bass of immense vigour and strength, which is repeated twice in F, and twice in B♭, during lines 3 and 4.

J. P. Sweelinck (same work).

etc.

The whole passage is repeated literally in B flat (a fourth higher), thus preparing the way for a "Plagal" Cadence, which brings the piece to an end.

Students of composition and of the history of "school" counterpoint will be delighted with the second bar of p. 31 :—

J. P. Sweelinck (same work).

which shows with beautiful clearness that the great Netherlander of the 16th century cared no more than J. S. Bach in the 18th century for consecutive octaves and fifths, if they interfered with his plans. Here are six of each sort, one for each accent of the bar.

All that is necessary has now been said about the "Hexachord" pieces in the Fitzwilliam Book. They show very clearly the essential difference in the notion of a "Scale" which the classical 16th century held, as compared with that which obtained only a few years later, viz., that their scale was Ut, Re, Mi, Fa, Sol, La, and did not essentially include the remaining two notes.

They also help to show that certain musicians of the 16th and early 17th centuries had a system of tuning not far different from the "equal" temperament which we now use for all keyed instruments, viz., neither "just" nor "mean-tone" tuning, but a compromise, in which all the twelve semitones in the octave are "equal" in magnitude.

But the most important thing is the witness borne in them to the new growth of harmonic modulation, or, in other words, the growth of the motion of "Key," which eventually destroyed the Modes of the Middle Ages, and the appearance of which marks the beginning of modern music.

In this connection, the following list of references in the Fitzwilliam Virginal Book, which seem to supply evidence on the question, may be useful to the student.

List of References in the Fitzwilliam Virginal Book, of possible evidence as to a growing sense of "Key," as distinguished from "Modal" transition, or chromatic alteration, in the music of the 16th century.

Bull, i. 183. F to Db, p. 184, l. 5.

E major to Db, p. 183, l. 5. (Bull's methods ruthless.)

Byrd, i. 395. p. 397, ll. 3, 4, 5, G to G minor, C minor, C major.

i. 401. ? Key of D major, p. 401, l. 4. (Byrd musical.)

Tisdall, ii. 278. ? Key of B major or thereabouts. p. 280, l. 2, etc. good :

ii. 307. G minor. p. 308, a great struggle for something, difficult to describe.

Hooper, ii. 309. A major, most of first half, and *all* second half. (See above, p. 31.)

Sweelinck, ii. 31. ? Eb. Not convincing, probably merely the result of the Hexachordal repetition.

Warrock, i. 389. ? Minor "scale" (chords of).

i. 384. ? Bb major.

Anon., ii. 312. E major, with Tonic, Dominant, Subdominant, quite plain in first section only. (See below, p. 131.)

Oystermayre, ii. 405. G major, real " modulations " in line 3. One of the most likely cases. Section 2 goes through D major, A major, E major, B minor, F♯ minor, etc. (See above, p. 22.)

Giles Farnaby, ii. 270, bottom line to top of p. 271. G. D, A, E, B, and back to C. But this seems to be a 'result of taking Ut, Re, Mi, Fa, four times up. (See the bass of the passage, and tenor of the first two quavers on p. 271.)

Anon., ii. 375. N.B.—The Alman on ii. 375 is a useful example of what distinctly *Modal harmony* is, and the hopeless difference between that and our modern sequence of chords is felt easily. Even playing over the *tune* alone, simple as it is, shows the distinction. See below, p. 138.

Giles Farnaby, ii. 17. " Pawles Wharfe." This tune is certainly in D major. Tonic, Subdominant, Dominant.

Robert Johnson, ii. 159. Alman, in D major. Tonic and Dominant, quite strong. An excellent case. A beautiful and graceful tune. (See below, p. 137.) The copy is incorrect at l. 2, bar 2, where the tenor should be e d *e* (minim); also in l. 4, bar 2, where an alto part is badly missing, viz., from the third crotchet, g f♯ e (minim), in tenths with the low tenor.

Richard Farnaby, ii. 162, 163. " Nobody's Gigge," in C. A quite useful instance. Tonic and Dominant.

CHAPTER XI

It is now necessary to put together the materials available in the Fitzwilliam Virginal Book for a chapter on the state of English music in the latter half of the 16th century.

The collection is most interesting to the student of musical history, containing, as it does, so many examples of every kind of music that was current during the Tudor Period in England.

We have here nearly 300 pieces of music by over 30 composers of that period. Thus the collection is more correctly regarded as a library than as a mere book, for it contains more direct evidence of the musical practice of the Tudor times than most of us have of the music of our own century, as any reader may prove to himself by honestly enumerating the composers of the 19th century whose names he knows, and such of their works as he can call to mind.

A thorough knowledge of the contents of this " book," especially when accompanied by contemporary illustrations in other forms (e.g., the original Madrigals, of which "arrangements" are found in the Fitzwilliam Book), would entitle a musician of a critical turn to an opinion as to the state of composition in Elizabeth's time, the main conclusions whereof would be second in value to none that we have been able to secure for the more recent centuries where so much larger quantities of material are at hand.

The first thing that looms large on the student of the Fitzwilliam Book is the " dead end " at which the " classical " train had brought up about the year 1600.

We consider the Dances, especially the Pavans and Galliards, and the numerous Songs, which have received the adornment of variations for the delight of the virginal player of the Elizabethan day, and what do we find?

At once we must honestly say, that on a broad inspection of the very large number of specimens of this sort of thing, it is only clear that none of these excellent composers could think what to do next in the direction of Variation of Melody. It is all *agrémens*, and everybody does it alike. A few examples suffice for the whole to be fairly appraised.*

---

* One example, of a very limited number, where a "variation" is achieved without simple ornamentation of the melody, or contrapuntal imitation of the melody, is the fourth variation on "The Woods so Wild," by William Byrd. The plain tune is to be found below, p. 145, and the student will observe that the fourth variation scarcely *alludes* to the tune, but builds an imitative passage taken from it, *on to the same harmonies* which are set to the original melody.

FOURTH VARIATION ON "THE WOODS SO WILD," by W. Byrd (i. 263).
See below, p. 145.

Here we see that although the rhythmical figure is got from bar 2 of the original tune, the tune itself is disregarded. The extract is also useful as showing the time signature 3, meaning here $\frac{6}{4}$ or $\frac{12}{4}$; the irregular use of bar lines; and the absence of the flat in the signature, where the modern ear

There are only a few hints in the book that even the best of the Tudor composers had any idea of "Development" in the sense that has been the common ground of the best writing since their day ; but those few hints are very valuable to the student ; slight as they are, they contain the germ of new life.

FORM (External).

The most important of these may be directly named ; it is, that the theory and the practice of the time agreed in supposing that the Galliard *en suite* might be made from the same melody and harmony as its proper Pavan, with the necessary alterations induced by the change to triple rhythm from quadruple. This is, of course, a perfect, though simple, case of pure modern "Development."

And equally, of course, any fool can "play upon this pipe," when he has once been shown how ; so let us not forget to thank our Tudor forebears for a method that has helped to make Brahms a possibility, three centuries after their time.

Some examples are as follows :—

Edward Johnson, ii. 436 and 440. A striking case, where *all the three sections* of the Pavan are paralleled in the Galliard following it.

FIRST "STRAIN" OF PAVANA (DELIGHT)
(FITZWILLIAM BOOK, ii. 436).

EDWARD JOHNSON (Elizabethan).

would (at least in bar 1) diagnose the key of F. (Of course the piece is not in a "key" at all ; see elsewhere.)

First "Strain" of Galiarda (belonging to, and made from the Pavana), Fitzwilliam Book, ii. 440.

In these examples the corresponding chords in the Galliard and Pavana are marked with the same letters of the alphabet.

Ferdinando Richardson, i. 27 and 32.

Dr Bull, i. 131, and the Pavan belonging to it, which is in *Parthenia*, published 1611 (see i. 234, which is practically the same).

Peter Philips, i. 299 and 306, where several sections in Pavana and Galliard are clearly parallel.

Also *Byrd's* Passamezzo Pavana and Galiarda, i. 203, 209; and *Philips'* Pavana Paggett and Galiard, i. 291, 296.

The practice was, however, by no means universal. Still, it was not uncommon.

The arrangement of Pavan and Galliard with a Preludium preceding them, which seems to have been done "on purpose" by the compiler of Parthĕnia, "the first virginal music ever printed" (1611), appears to indicate that the notion of a "Suite" extended even further than the mere relation of Pavan and Galliard. This again is an undoubted hint of the future possibility of the Dance-named Suite of the early 18th century, and thus of the Sonata and Symphony of several movements, which is still the noblest achievement of pure music in the 20th century.

Form (Internal).

Another sign of undeveloped life, a few instances of which are to be found in these pieces, is the attempt at Internal Unity in certain of the Dance Tunes, by Repetition of some kind, apart from " variation."

As we know already, the interesting beginnings of certain well-established features of modern " Form" are plainly seen in some quite ancient melodies, e.g., church plain songs, which now and then show a tendency to "repeat" a portion of the tune at the end which has already appeared nearer the beginning. An instance is " Ein' Feste Burg," the last line of which is a literal repetition of the second line. Another example is " Christe Redemptor," quoted further on, p. 176. Also, for a secular case, compare the Fitzwilliam Book, ii. 162 and 163 ("Nobody's Gigge," by R. Farnaby).

This is very elementary in appearance, but it is doubtless the germ of the great principle which underlies at once the most cut-and-dried formula of a second-rate 18th century Sonata and the apparent rhapsody of the 20th century Ballade or Tone-picture. None of them has yet succeeded without this principle of Repetition in some shape.

Accordingly, so far back as the 16th century, we find the principle already (if not recognised in theory, still) adopted in the practice of composers.

We may give as an example "Mal Sims," a Pavan, i. 68 or ii. 448 (where the same tune is varied by Giles Farnaby). In this Pavan, which is Binary in form, like most Sonata movements up to our own time, we find the main features of the first half reproduced or alluded to in the second half, and it is hardly too much to say that this 16th century melody is a more creditable specimen of coherent form than many a Sonata movement of two centuries later. It even corresponds to the most modern form, in the introduction of something like a "free" section (p. 69, last two bars of the top line and first two bars of line 2), which makes the second half longer than the first, thus weighting it suitably and convincing the hearer of a conclusion.

MAL SIMS (FITZWILLIAM VIRGINAL BOOK, i. 68 AND ii. 447).

[*A song, in Pavan form.*]

Brightly, but not too fast.

The final two bars are in the most intimate connection with
the first and last bars of the first strain. The one bar tends
towards the "Dominant," the other towards the "Tonic,"
so that, in a limited sense, the first and second "subjects"
of modern works are exemplified on a small scale. The
rhythmical character also of bars 1 and 2 of the second strain
is precisely that of the corresponding bars of the first strain.
The low pitch of bar 2, in the second strain, is an echo to
the similar passage in line 1, bar 3. The two bars marked
by round brackets are what I refer to as the "free" portion.

Other instances are :—ii. 188, La Volta (*i.e.* the "high
lavolt," or quick Galliard, in which the "caper" was the

main feature), a tune by *Morley*, and arranged by *Byrd*. This short piece is frankly in G major. The first half begins on the Tonic and ends on the Dominant; the second half favours the Dominant, and ends on the Tonic. The main lines of the "Old Binary" form had not gone beyond this 16th century example under Bach in the 18th century. *Bull's* "Gigge" (ii. 258) has much the same features, and another good case is "Pawles Wharfe" (ii. 17), set by *Giles Farnaby*, already mentioned as plainly showing the Tonic, Subdominant, and Dominant chords of the "Key" of D major. The final two bars of the second half are the same as the corresponding part of the first half, but the sequence of keys does not include a modulation to the Dominant at the end of the first half (see below, p. 134).

Another, and in some respects even a better, instance is the Alman (ii. 375), which is strictly Binary in form, and has the latter half of the first section reproduced literally (except for an ornament of semiquavers in one bar) in the latter half of the second section. (The second section also begins on a chord of the "dominant" key, if one may use the term here; but I do not lay any stress on this feature.) This work, however, as has already been mentioned, is altogether "Modal" in its harmonies, and is to be thought of, not as in a "key" of G, but as in the Mixolydian Mode.

Similar coherence, in a probably older tune, may be observed in "Walsingham" (i. 1, or i. 267). Short as it is, the second four bars depend wholly on the first four, as is easily seen.

"WALSINGHAM" (early 16th Century, at latest).

1. As ye came from the Ho - - - ly Land

2. How should I know your true love,

(Words: Percy Folio, vol. iii. 471.)

To speak in our modern way, this " Walsingham " has two bars in A minor, and then two bars in C major (the relative major of A minor). Here ends the first section. This sequence of keys was not improved upon in Beethoven three centuries later. The second section, as may be seen by mere inspection, is formed entirely on the model furnished by the first section, with the two interesting alterations—(1) the line begins on B instead of C, thus indicating a harmony of E major (what we now call the "dominant" of A minor); and (2) the last two bars are altered so as to finish, not in C major, as the first line did, but in A major itself. Thus the key sequence, and the interdependence of the different portions of the tune, almost perfectly correspond with the practice of the 19th century.

The "Duke of Brunswick's Alman" (ii. 146) should be compared with "Walsingham," partly because the curious change (curious to *our* ears) from minor to major, in the last phrase, occurs in both. This is not to be considered as a peculiarity of Bull, simply because both pieces have his name. Byrd has the same thing in *his* setting of " Walsingham," i. 267; also G. Farnaby, ii. 19, line 3, last bar. But the " Duke of Brunswick's Alman " is more valuable, as another good example of interdependence between the sections of a Binary movement. So complete is it in this case, that the 3rd and 4th bars of Section I. can almost be played together with the corresponding bars of Section II., in spite of the tune and bass differing considerably.

The same thing can nearly be said of the 1st and 2nd bars in each section. At least, they are connected most intimately in their harmonic tendencies.

These specimens are sufficient in number, and, I think, quite convincing.

DEVELOPMENT.

The next point is, that " symptoms " of the simpler notions of " Development," as used in modern writings, are to be seen in another anonymous Alman (i. 65), containing *three* sections (3 sections is the most common arrangement in these old dances), the 3rd of which introduces two phrases, the first of *two* " bars," which is used again in " sequence," a tone higher ; the second being a shorter phrase of *one* " bar," which is doubled on itself by ornamental repetition, and then repeated in sequence like the first, thus producing a section of *ten* " bars," a mighty contrast with the former two divisions of the whole movement, which have only *eight* " bars " (the most usual number).

MELODY OF THE 3RD "STRAIN" OF AN ALMAN
(FITZWILLIAM BOOK, i. 65).

ANON. (16th Century).

Here are 10 "bars" instead of the regular 8.

Bars 1 and 2, founded on a chord of F major, are used in sequence to produce bars 3 and 4, founded on a chord of G minor.

Bars 5 and 6 (harmony of C major) are similarly made to give forth bars 7 and 8 (harmony of D major); and thus the piece presents a somewhat advanced case of development of phrases, resulting in the lengthening of the whole division.

The student will carefully note that the signature of one flat merely indicates that the Dorian Mode has suffered "transposition," *i.e.* that the notes of that mode have been raised in pitch from D up to G, a perfect fourth, according to the practice of the time. The piece is *not* in what we call G minor, though we probably should consider its general character to be fairly indicated by that name.

A nice instance of a similar "development" is in ii. 405, section 2, of Oystermayre's Galiard.

SECOND "STRAIN" OF JEHAN OYSTERMAYRE'S GALIARDA
(FITZWILLIAM BOOK, ii. 405).

(16th Century.)

The characteristic motive of this example, taken from the *second* strain, appears in bar 3 of the *first* strain; moreover, another sequence is found in the *third* strain, the melody of which seems to be a sort of "development" of the melody in the first bars of the first strain. Thus the solitary specimen of Oystermayre's work which is given in the Fitzwilliam Virginal Book, may be regarded as a particularly remarkable example of modern tendencies (also see below, p. 139, and above, p. 22, where the whole piece is given).

A final instance may be taken of William Tisdall's "Pavana Chromatica," where (ii. 280, lines 2 and 3) a phrase is repeated in ascending sequence in three successive bars, and even a fourth bar is made by the same trick, in a less complete form.

Thus we are able to point out slight but quite unmistakable evidences that English (and other, *e.g.*, German) composers of the 16th century were striving, darkly but surely, after three main features of modern music :—

(1) Coherence, by means of "formal" repetition.
(2) Development of melody by *agrémens*, by altered rhythm, or by sequence.
(3) The larger Coherence of a series of movements *en suite*, from which we derive Symphony, Sonata, Quartet, etc.

THE NEW MATERIALS.

It is plain that a considerable growth in the method of Instrumental Music might have taken place on the general lines which are indicated in these three main orders, quite apart from any startling change in the simple materials of music, the Melody, the Harmonies, or the scales to which these last are referred. For this reason I have noticed first the three features named above.

The modes clearly did not *prevent* the practice of tune, chord, or design, in music.

But, with the close of the Tudor period, we notice that great changes are at hand in other matters besides those of melody, harmony, or form.

The "ecclesiastical" influence was dying down, and the "secular" characteristics of the music of the people were on the eve of asserting themselves, in a more positive manner than had hitherto been possible to ages which reckoned the "secular" musician no better than a jack-pudding or common street tumbler, who varied his witticisms or acrobatisms with fiddling or piping of "Dances" and "Gigges."

It was beginning to appear to composers in general that contrapuntal exercises were not inexhaustible fountains of inspiration. Thus they tried "variations" on well-known melodies. Later on they found those melodies to contain within themselves the possibilities of spontaneous growth, the most complete exemplification of which we now possess, three hundred years later, in (say) Brahms's Violin Sonatas.

Now, what *were* the "secular characteristics of the music of the people," mentioned above?

We have already seen some of them in the simple cheerfulness and artistic coherence of the anonymous Dance tunes which are to be found in the Fitzwilliam Virginal Book. They depend on rhythm and natural tunefulness, not upon harmony, whether attained "accidentally" by contrapuntal setting, or by design of bass and super-imposed chord. They are constructed on a plan that knows more about the Tabor-pipe than of the Schoolmen's Modes; more about the modern Scale of eight notes than of the *Hexachordum Durum*; more of natural Accent than of the "Proportions" enumerated by Gaffurius (1496). (The hopeless character of some of these "Proportions" is excellently demonstrated by Dr John Bull's experiments, *e.g.*, i. 186, 187; ii. 66; ii. 39, line 2, bar 2, etc.)

It is easy to show how little in common these "popular"

melodies have with those of the Church. The following may be confidently referred to as specimens of no uncommon order, which will convince any one that it was not the nature of the words only which made the difference between sacred and secular music in the 16th century.

LIST OF EXAMPLES of secular tunes in the Fitzwilliam Virginal Book, which show modern tendencies of Scale or Key.

1. " Jhon come kisse me now," set by *Byrd,* i. 47.
2. " Nancie," set by *Morley,* i. 57 ; affected by Mode, however.
3. Pavana, by *Bull,* i. 62 ; except the *chord* of F in bar 2.
4. Muscadin, *Anon.* } i. 74, 75. Parts of these.
5. Alman,   *Anon.* }
6. Galliard, " St Thomas Wake," *Bull,* i. 131.
7. " The King's Hunt," set by *Giles Farnaby,* i. 196.
8. Spagnioletta, set by *Giles Farnaby,* i. 199.
9. " The Carman's Whistle," set by *Byrd,* i. 214.
10 " Now God be with old Simeon," introduced by *Byrd* in his " Hunt's up," i. 223.
11. " O Mistris Myne," set by *Byrd,* i. 258.
    (Compare the *tune* of " Woods so wilde," p. 263, and see how great the difference.)
12. " Pawles Wharf," set by *G. Farnaby,* ii. 17 ; positively in the Key of D major. A good piece.
    (Compare " Pawles Wharf" with " Quodling's Delight," p. 19, and observe the contrast.)
13. Alman, by *Robert Johnson,* ii. 159; in D major.
14. " Nobody's Gigge," *Richard Farnaby,* ii. 162, 163; in C major.
15. Alman, *Thomas Morley,* ii. 171 ; in key of C. Tonic, subdominant, and dominant quite clear.

16. La Volta, *Byrd*, ii. 180, in G. (Compare with Alman, p. 182.)

17. La Volta, *Morley*, arr. by Byrd, ii. 188. In G, with "modulation" to D. The "Form" very nearly Modern Binary.

18. Lady Zouches Maske, G. *Farnaby*, ii. 350.

19. "Tower Hill," G. *Farnaby*, ii. 371.

20. The Earle of Oxford's Marche, *Byrd*, ii. 402. In G, D, and G.

21. The Old Spagnoletta, G. *Farnaby*, ii. 471 ; in " G minor," with "relative" major, "dominant" major, and return to " G minor."

N.B.—With the exception of these twenty or so pieces, all of which are "popular" in character, the Fitzwilliam Virginal Book simply shows that the Modes reigned very completely in the minds of musicians as late at least as the year 1600.

We can now add something to our former proposal, and may, with some confidence, hold an opinion that the " Music of the People," in the 16th century, as shown in the Fitzwilliam Book, was in favour of—

(1) The adoption of the Major and Minor SCALES, instead of the Hexachords.

(2) The adoption of KEYS, instead of the Modes.

(3) The use of the characteristic CHORDS of the Key, as we now understand them, namely the TONIC, SUBDOMINANT, and DOMINANT.

(4) The composition of melodies in BINARY FORM, with internal unity of the keys and of the constituent sentences, corresponding very nearly with the general features of a Beethoven Sonata movement two centuries later.

But, as with other great changes, the transition to modern ways was effected gently, and without any alarming explosion on the part of the talkers. This kingdom also came " not with observation."

Even now, in spite of all that has been written since the time of Henry VIII., the Modes are still with us. Every time Tallis's " Festal Responses " are sung in church, we hear how impossible it is to put entirely away from us this ancient practice of harmony.

In our own time alone, leaving out all mention of the centuries between, Dvorák and Verdi, Wagner and others, cannot, under certain circumstances, refrain from using chords in series, which owe their grandeur even more to the continuous tradition of the familiar things of the 15th and 16th centuries, than to their intrinsic worth, high though that may be.

" Parsifal " alone is enough to prove this point, to any student who knows that work as it should be known.

" Pièces Justificatives."

It will not be improper here to consider, with some care, certain examples in the Fitzwilliam Book which may be regarded as the " pièces justificatives " of my case.

Bull's very remarkable experiment on the Hexachord (i. 183) supplies us with some examples of " modulation " which are quite outside the regular practice of his time, and which (as we have seen) can be regarded as successful in a somewhat modified degree. Nevertheless, as already has been pointed out, Bull's general characteristics make it right to suspect (not his bonâ fides, but) a certain measure of insincerity in the production of this work. If Bull's work stood alone, it could hardly be accepted as a proof that " enharmonic modulation " and " equal temperament " formed part of the direct heritage of the 17th century. But it does not stand alone.

William Byrd's exercise on the same theme (Hexachord)

is thoroughly characteristic of the composer, and furnishes a much-needed foil to the work of Bull. Byrd is always *a musician first*, and a technician afterwards if he feels inclined.

The signs of his utter unwillingness to be ugly because his first plan leads logically to ugliness, are plain all through his works, whether in the Fitzwilliam Book or elsewhere : i. 397, line 3 onwards, shows us the way from G major to G minor and C minor, but in the spirit of the true composer, not of the teacher of Harmony.

In spite of the innocent ease of these " transitions " of Byrd's, they are, to my mind, more really to be regarded as evidence of Byrd's growing feeling for " Key " as opposed to " Mode," than Bull's more complete and startling efforts.

Bull, in fact, behaves like his namesake in the china shop, and sends everything flying that he can get his horns anywhere near. As I have said before, he is a " ruthless " artist.

Byrd, on the other hand, has the gentleness which makes for beauty; and he cares for beauty equally with progress, though he was by no means a Church and State Tory, but, on the contrary, a Roman Catholic Nonconformist who gave some trouble to the authorities in his time.

Clearly, the evidence of the growth of the new methods is greatly strengthened when two men of such widely contrasted tendencies show themselves at work in the same direction.

Nor are these two giant explorers alone in their newly discovered country.

William Tisdall may perhaps have doubt cast upon his use as a witness to the facts. The Pavana Chromatica, ii. 278, is very full of sharps and of semitonal progressions (line 2), but, the student might object, it is Modal after all in character. So it is; and what else could be expected! Take the reverse case. Set a man, born in the 19th century, to imitate the Modal progressions of the 16th century. In spite of an immense knowledge of all the particulars of the difference between the one style and the other, every line of his production betrays him. Every line speaks loud of the later period, and the work does not even deceive the expert of to-day, still less could it have deceived those of the earlier time, in whose atmosphere it vainly seeks to breathe again.

Well may we find that Tisdall and his contemporaries of the Elizabethan time, with *no* complete prophetic knowledge of what was to come, indeed with only a dim shadowy notion that anything new *could* come, do as a rule fail in their efforts to leave behind them the old practices which they seem to have felt were becoming insufficient for their needs.

But Tisdall's Chromatic Pavan is of great value for our purpose, if we care to remember that parts of it (*e.g.*, section I) require as many as four sharps (*i.e.* those of the key of E major); that it begins and ends on a chord of B major, and constantly uses that chord, so unusual to the age in which this piece was written; and that on the other hand, the second section is entirely in the Mixolydian mode, requiring only *one* sharp note. We cannot suppose that Tisdall was otherwise than gratified at his work, or that he was less than pleased to find that the harmony of B major was so nearly related to that of G.

The same piece, p. 280, lines 2 and 3, affords a good "sequence" of four bars, in which the harmonies are successively G major, E minor, D major, B major.

In a Pavana, ii. 307, Tisdall appears at first to be aiming at the scale of G minor; while on p. 308 there is manifestly a great struggle towards something which is scarcely well enough defined to receive the name of "Modulation."

The passage from Sweelinck's "Ut Re Mi Fa Sol La"

(the date, 1612,* may be the year when the piece was *copied* by the writer of the Fitzwilliam Virginal Book), vol. ii. p. 31, where there is apparently a "modulation" from the region of F major to A minor and to E flat, is, I fear, merely a formal consequence of the subject on which the piece is written.

A similar remark applies to Giles Farnaby's apparent progress through the keys of G D A E B, and back to C, in ii. 270, bottom line to top of next page. This is only the result of writing *Ut, Re, Mi, Fa* four times over in scale form, and then adding upper parts to it (p. 270, last bar,

* It would appear, however, that the dates given to certain of the works in the MS. are the dates of their composition.

The following short list of such dates seems to make this plain :—

Reference in the printed copy of the MS.	Date given.	Name of Composer (or arranger).
i. 266	1590 (the first date in the book)	Byrd
i. 305	1592	Philips
i. 320	1602	Philips
i. 326	1593	Philips
i. 331	1603	Philips
i. 334	1605	Philips
i. 345	1580	"Philips' first"
i. 350	1545	Philips
i. 356	1582	Philips
i. 436	1562 (the earliest date in the book)	Tallis
ii. 11	1564	Tallis
ii. 33	1612	Sweelinck

Other more or less "datable" pieces are—

ii. 273, a "Maske" ascribed to G. Farnaby, which appears to have been a dance in a Gray's Inn Masque in 1613 (viz., The Maske of Flowers) bearing the name of Coperario. See above, p. 7.

ii. 330, G. Farnaby's arrangement of his own "Canzonet," "Ay me poor heart," date 1598.

i. 131, Bull's Galliard "St Thomas Wake," which was published (with its Pavan) in 1611 (Parthenia), and

ii. 479, Gibbons' Pavana (Æolian), also in Parthenia, 1611.

tenor, affords another instance of the uncertain notation of such passages : E♭ for D♯).

On the other hand, the anonymous Alman, ii. 312, is written (at least in the first " strain ") definitely in the " Key " of E major. (The author, of course, knew of no such term, but he clearly knew the thing signified by the term.) It is useful to contrast the 2nd and 3rd strains with the 1st in this case. The little piece is so interesting that I give it complete.

ALMAN (Fitzwilliam Virginal Book, ii. 312).
[*Piece No.* 227.]

* The alto part is slightly corrected here, and the uniformity of the syncopated imitation preserved.

In this one short piece the student may see illustrated several of the characteristic features of the clavier music of the 16th century, *e.g.*—

(*a*) The notation. Although the four sharps of the " key "

of E are wanted everywhere, they are written throughout as "accidentals."

(*b*) The straightforward construction of the work, in three strains, each consisting of eight semibreves.

(*c*) The irregular use of bars, some containing 4 crotchets, others 8 crotchets.

(*d*) The fashion of playing the chord of the "key" at the end of the piece, reminding one of the Wiltshire (and other) countrymen who invariably announce the title of the song they have just sung, before sitting down.

(*e*) Most important of all, the mixture of "modal" harmony and "modal" tune with "scale" harmony and "scale" tune, *e.g.*, the first strain, entirely in the modern "key" of E major; the second strain altogether "modal," whether the chords or the melody itself are considered; the third strain, where (in the last line) the immense difficulty of persuading the music to return to the "key" of E major is very strangely shown.

(*f*) The extreme compass of the Elizabethan virginals (as given in the Fitzwilliam Book) is found in this piece, viz., 4 clear octaves, from A under the bass staff, to *a* over the treble staff.

After contrasting the 2nd and 3rd strains of the above Alman with the 1st strain, and noticing the essential differences, the reader should play through the Alman (anonymous), ii. 375 (see below, p. 138), which is "modal" in tune and harmony alike, and contrast it also with "Pawles Wharfe," ii. 17, by Giles Farnaby. The latter is as certainly in the "key" of D major as can possibly be: the Tonic, Subdominant, and Dominant characteristics are plainly present, and are used in order, just as we have been accustomed to them now for many years back.

Equally certain is it, that "Quodling's Delight" (G. Farnaby again), ii. 19, is *not* in the modern "Key" of A

minor. As will be perceived, it is founded on the notes
la, sol, la, mi, which are characteristic of many early "modal"
tunes.

It is of the greatest consequence to the student that he
should have a clear idea of the distance between these two
methods of harmony; therefore I here give these two tunes,
shorn of repetitions.

"PAWLES WHARFE" (FITZWILLIAM BOOK, ii. 17).

[*16th century example of the modern "key" of D major, with its
essential harmonies of Tonic, Dominant, Sub-dominant.*]

GILES FARNABY.

Here in section 1 we have a tune made of the plain " scale " of D major, accompanied by " tonic " and " dominant " chords in such order as modern ears have come to expect. In section 2, bar 1, we find the " subdominant " chord (of G) introduced in such a manner as to emphasise it as a characteristic of the " key."

On the other hand, " Quodling's Delight," set by the same composer, is definitely wanting in certain features of our modern " minor scale," and is definitely *not* wanting in the characteristics of " modal " harmony, *e.g.*, the basis La, Sol, La, Mi, which constantly appears in Æolian melodies.

"Quodling's Delight" (Fitzwilliam Book, ii. 19).

[*Showing " Modal" characteristics.*]

GILES FARNABY.

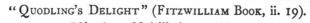

The "modal" basis is well seen in section 1, marked by capitals under the music. Had this piece been as truly in the modern "minor scale" of A, as the former ("Pawles Wharfe") is truly in the modern "major scale" of D, we should have perhaps found A E F E in place of A G A E. The general resemblance of the Æolian mode to the modern minor scale is no doubt striking; how otherwise! for in it we have the lineal progenitor of all modern minor scales; but in particulars the difference is very plain. The "essential" nature of the *G natural* in bar 1 should be compared with the "accidental" nature of the *G sharp* in bar 2. The one is of "Mode," the other of "Harmony." But in the "key" of A minor, *both* would be alike. Thus the distinction is clear, even to modern ears.

This piece is almost the same as "Fayne would I wedd," ascribed to Richard Farnaby, Giles's son (ii. 263).

Robert Johnson's Alman, ii. 159, a beautiful and graceful dance, furnishes an excellent instance of the strength of Tonic and Dominant in the "key" of D major; and Richard Farnaby's "Nobody's Gigge," ii. 162, 163, is quite as clearly in the key of C, with the Tonic and Dominant harmony plainly recognised.

Here is Johnson's piece :—

ALMAN (FITZWILLIAM BOOK, ii. 159).

Not too fast

ROBERT JOHNSON.

The final chord is a formality, as has already been observed. The probable alto part between * and * has been restored, and an obvious mistake in the tenor part of the final bar of the first strain corrected.

We remark in this Alman, (*a*) the "key" of D major, with scarcely a hint of the smallest kind that Robert Johnson lived amongst the Modes. (*b*) The chords of the Tonic, Subdominant, and Dominant throughout, used as they were used a century later, *e.g.*, bar 1, where all three occur in an order very familiar to modern hearers. (*c*) The modern touch of " Form," at the beginning of the second " strain," where a " free " section is actually modelled on the opening bars of the first " strain," just as it would be in a 19th century sonata movement.

The student may now turn back to the anonymous Alman (above, p. 131), and compare the 2nd and 3rd divisions of it with this of Johnson. A good experimental way of realising the abyss which lies between " Mode " and " Key " would be, to play over the first strain of Johnson's Alman, and then, while its general character is fresh in the memory, play the third strain of the anonymous Alman (above, p. 132), which begins on a chord (A major) closely related with the key of Johnson's piece, but leads to a very different sort of conclusion.

If this is not sufficient, the reader may play again the first strain of Johnson, and contrast with it the following two bars of another Alman (ii. 375), which has already been named more than once as having the Modal character strongly marked,

ALMAN (SHOWING " MODAL " HARMONY).

ANON. (16th century).

The difference between this "Modal" harmonisation and the harmony of modern "key" is seen as follows :—

THE SAME MELODY (SHOWING "KEY" HARMONY OF G MAJOR).

[With Signature.]

etc.

One chord only (marked *) is altered, but that is more than enough.

One of the most convincing specimens, however, is the Galiarda of Jehan Oystermayre, ii. 405, in which the Tonic, Subdominant, and Dominant are well marked in the key of G major; and (in the second "strain"), a sequential passage (quoted above, p. 122) leads the music naturally and pleasantly through D major, A major, B minor, D major, E, and back to D. Moreover, the general key effect in the three sections is, as in a modern work it would, or might easily, be, viz., G—; D—; G—. (See p. 22, where the whole piece is given.)

It is a pity more of this composer's works did not reach Mr Tregian.

A final example is that of Thomas Warrock (organist of Hereford, 1586), whose Pavana, i. 384, and Galiarda, i. 388, besides showing smoothness and grace beyond most of the music of the time, gives us some hope that the composer believed in the scale and key of B flat, and (in the Galiarda) even in the possibility of certain Minor Chords in the key of C major (p. 389, top line).

It is indeed possible to say that Thomas Warrock's signature of two flats is merely an indication of "Double Transposition"; but to call a piece Ionian does not do away with its general characteristics, and these seem to be decidedly separate from Mode, and equally akin to the idea of Key.

We have now seen practically *all* that can be found in this large collection of nearly 300 pieces, in the way of evidence for the early growth of modern methods of composition in the later 16th century.

It must not be pressed too far, but I venture to think that it will not be possible to reject most of it.

When all deductions are made, it seems clear to me that the idea of major and minor scale, of key, and of the characteristic chords of a key, *was* gaining recognition in England and the Netherlands about the time of Elizabeth, and that the germs of modern composition, in all essentials, were to be seen developing in the practice of that time.

CHAPTER XII

IT will now be interesting to look *backwards* from the Fitz-william Virginal Book, and to study some pieces in it which seem to have a relationship with the earliest Western Harmony, *i.e.* which appear to contain relics of the Origins of Harmony as it was already practised in the 12th century in England.

Some references to passages of this nature are: i. 54; i. 263; i. 42; i. 47; ii. 128; ii. 387; ii. 422.

Before looking at these the reader's attention must be directed to a peculiarity of many of the most ancient popular English melodies (which are often either Dorian or Æolian), namely, that they are founded on a simple "burden" (*bourdon*, drone, "buzzing bass"), consisting of two alternating notes, adjacent to each other.

Sometimes these are what we should call the first and second notes of the scale, as in the case of "Sumer is icumen in" (13th century), which has this characteristic, and any person may join in it by merely singing F G, F G, F G, etc., throughout as a sort of Ground Bass.

CANON ON "BURDEN" OF 13TH CENTURY.

141

In the actual work itself, which requires 6 voices (4 to the tune in Canon, and 2 to the " Pes " or " Pedal part "), the " burden " is given in a slightly more elaborate shape, the F G, F G, appearing first in one of the two " Pedal " voices and then in the other. But the gist of the thing is accurately represented in the above example, which shows that the writer of the 13th century had two chords in his mind. Here it is by no means trivial or without occasion to remind the reader that the common street accordion preserves this ancient feature, and that the players of this barbarous instrument do still try to fit the tunes they know on to the two chords which are at their disposal, according as the bellows are blown inwards or outwards.

The same remarks apply to a very old catch, " Heigh ho, nobody at home," where it is only necessary to alternate A G, A G (supposing it to be Æolian), in order to " take part " effectually.

CATCH ON " BURDEN," OF EARLY DATE.

(Date probably early 16th century.)

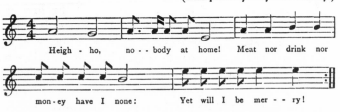

Here are 5 bars, and 5 voices may take part in the Canon of this catch, each beginning a bar after the other. The result, in harmony, is simply the alternation of two chords—

and, as will be seen, the two notes, A G, A G, can be continually alternated throughout.

Another case of a Northern tune, which has this characteristic, may not be so well known, though many country people still sing it in Yorkshire and Cumberland to a set of humorous words, beginning "When a liv'd at yam wi' ma fadher an' mudher," etc. The tune is Æolian in its tonality. A sufficient specimen is the chorus (transposed to a lower pitch for convenience, so that the burden A G A becomes D C D).

ANCIENT NORTH ENGLISH SONG ON "BURDEN"
(Cumberland and elsewhere).

Those who are not used to dialect may be glad to know that "Reyt" is the correct Northern for "Right," and that "Aw" means "Oh."

The burden D C D, etc., is marked in capitals under the music, and it is extremely probable, if this melody ever was sung with an instrumental or vocal accompaniment, that this "burden" would have been regarded as the correct thing.

It is well to notice that alternative drones of this nature

were found in the Northumbrian bagpipe, which possessed an arrangement for changing the note of the drone or drones ; and that something of the same sort is still heard in the Italian bagpipe performance with two players, one of whom plays the tune on a "chanter," or rough kind of oboe, the other accompanying him on a larger instrument which supplies a limited pedal bass.

A few remarks on the possible connection of the ancient melody and harmony of the bagpipe, with the passages in the Fitzwilliam Virginal Book referred to above, will not be altogether out of place.

My suggestion is, that these ancient "burdens" of two alternating notes lie at the very root of the mediæval notion of Harmony (apart from the harmonies produced by Counterpoint, or the combining of melodies), and therefore that the student must regard any possible evidence as to their development with careful interest.

The first example is by Bull, the Galliard to my Lord Lumley's Pavan, i. 54. The tune of the first strain is remarkably like a real bagpipe tune *in every way*,* and a double drone-bass of the kind already described is indicated in the harmony given by Bull.

BULL (1563-1628.)

* A curious comparison may be drawn between this tune and the second section of the castanet song in Bizet's "Carmen," which is strangely like Bull's melody, and stands on an alternate drone bass of F G F G. See "Carmen," No. 17, the eight bars preceding the entry of the trumpets.

The most likely "burden" seems to be G and A, as marked. Another case is "Goe from my window" (i. 42) by Morley (or Munday), where the harmony is alternately based on G and A throughout.

Byrd gives us an instance in his "John come kiss me now" (i. 47), where the burden or "bussing bass" of G F G D, would be quite in character. Compare the burden of La, Sol, La, Mi (A G A E), which underlies the catch "Heigh ho, nobody at home," quoted above (p. 142).

The same composer harmonises "The Woods so Wild" (words unknown, see Chappell, i. 119) on practically two chords, those of F and G, thus—

"THE WOODS SO WILD" (FITZWILLIAM BOOK, i. 263).

[*Showing drone bass or burden.*]

WILLIAM BYRD (1538-1623).

Here we have F and G in alternate bars. But the student will carefully note that it is not the same case as that of "Sumer is icumen in" (p. 141 above), which is written in the key of the "softened B," or bémol, alluded to by Giraldus Cambrensis as being characteristic of the part singing in Northern England in his time (end of the 12th century).

Dr John Bull's "Juell" (ii. 128) is founded on the same bass as "Heigh ho," etc., only beginning on C, and using another order, viz., instead of C, B flat, C, G, it has C, G, B flat, C, etc., according to the demands of the tune. The second strain is even more convincing than the first.

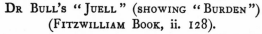

DR BULL'S "JUELL" (SHOWING "BURDEN")
(FITZWILLIAM BOOK, ii. 128).

First strain   JOHN BULL (1563-1628).

Second strain

N.B.—The minim note " g " in the left hand part of bar 4 in the second strain is probably an error for " b." Compare the variation which follows on p. 129, where the corresponding bar is founded entirely on Bb.

Byrd's Galiarda (ii. 387) has the word "Drone" as it were written on it in large letters. The first strain has, in common with other pieces already mentioned, the " burden" La, Sol, La, Mi (A G A E), as its harmonic basis.

Martin Peerson's " The Primerose " (ii. 422) is worth mentioning on account of the alterations of the chord of C with that of Bb, and back again, which may be seen in line 4 and onward.

A final instance is found in Peter Philips, the English Roman Catholic priest, who supplies us with a Passamezzo Galliard, *en suite* with the Passamezzo Pavan preceding it (dated 1592). The reference to the Galliard is i. 306, and the student will observe that the basis of the first four bars is G, F, G, D, *i.e.* once again, La, Sol, La, Mi.

These ten examples of "popular" harmony seem to point in one direction, and to indicate the source of chord music, by which I mean harmony which was *not* the result of "contrapuntal" combination.

In all likelihood they fairly represent the four centuries from John to James I. in this respect, and they certainly encourage the student in a belief that the modern notion of a "Bass," implying harmonies and implicit melody, is directly traceable to the drones of the bagpipe family.

PARTHENIA

or

THE MAYDENHEAD
of the first musicke that

ever was printed for the VIRGINALLS

COMPOSED

By three famous Masters William Byrd. D: John Bull & Orlando Gibbons.
Gentilmen of his Ma:ties most Illustrious Chappell

Ingrauen
by William Hole

Lond: print: for M. Dor: Euans. Cum priuilegio. Are to be sould by G.
Lowe printe in Loathberry

CHAPTER XIII

THE ELIZABETHAN VIRGINALS

THE clavier used by the Composers of the pieces in the Fitzwilliam Book was known as "the virginals." For the plural form of the word one may compare such cases as "scissors," or "bands" (the ecclesiastical neck-wear). It was common also to speak of "a *pair* of virginals," for which, again, we compare "a pair of scissors," "a pair of bands." The name itself seems to point to the domestic use of the instrument. It was in fact the ladies' clavier, and so got its graceful title. Shakespeare's "Winter's Tale" (i. 2, l. 125) gives us an instance of the name used as a verb, where Leontes the King of Sicilia speaks of Hermione and Polixenes—

> "still virginalling
> upon his palm?"

Thus, in Shakespeare's mind, the word "virginals" clearly pictured the action of musical fingers on a keyed instrument.

The "virginals" of the latter half of the 16th century had much in common with the harpsichord of later times. That is to say, it had a keyboard similar to that of our modern pianoforte, organ, or harmonium, but of short compass, viz., about four octaves at the most; it had wire strings, similar to those of the modern pianoforte, but very much thinner, shorter, and slacker.

The harpsichord, on the other hand, was made (as its name implies) in the shape of a harp (*i.e.* its ground plan

was much the same as that of the modern grand pianoforte);
whereas the "virginals" had a flat rectangular case like
that of the old-fashioned "square" piano.[1]

The grand difference between harpsichord and pianoforte
was, that whereas the action of the latter consists in the
striking of the strings with a *hammer*, the action of the harpsichord consisted in *plucking* the string with a *plectrum* (or
"spike" of quill, metal, or other suitable material).

The action of the 16th century virginals was essentially
the same as that of the 18th century harpsichord, that is,
each string was "plucked" by a horizontal plectrum carried
on a "jack" (a vertical slip of wood, moved upwards by the
far end of the key lever, and called "jack" because it spent
its life in "jigging" up and down in its groove). Thus the
quality of tone was not unlike that produced by the plectrum
of the mandoline on a *single string*. Also (more important
still), the virginals could make no difference whatever
between loud and soft, for the action could do no less and
would do no more than simply "pluck" the strings; thus,
however hard the blow administered by the player, no
"dynamic" expression whatever could be got out of the
instrument, which merely continued to produce an average
sort of mezzo-forte tone, louder or softer according to its
individual nature, but never altering.

We now proceed to gather together the information
respecting the "virginals" which can be found in the
Fitzwilliam Book, by a careful examination of the pieces
given in that MS.

In the first place, there was a variety of compass in these
old claviers of the Tudor times. (This was also the case
with the older pianofortes, *e.g.*, a little square piano by Zumpe
of London, dated 1766, has five octaves, less by one note,

---

[1] The virginals was described first by Virdung (Basel, 1511), who gives a
picture showing the rectangular form of the instrument.

beginning at G below the bass staff, whereas another old square by Wilson of Scarborough, dated 1791, has the full five octaves from FFF to f³. Even in our own time extensions of compass have been introduced.)

Peter Philips appears to have had an instrument with a

somewhat meagre-looking keyboard, viz., having [E] as its lowest key, and [A] for its topmost note. But Philips had other resources which do not meet the eye at the first inspection. His instrument was provided with the curious arrangement known as the " Short Octave," by which, although the keyboard came to an apparent end at

low E, the complete diatonic scale of C was available in the lowest octave. The idea was, that low F♯ and G♯ were seldom found, and therefore that their mechanism might as well be used for other notes.

The arrangement is best shown as follows :—

" SHORT OCTAVE."

Notes actually
  played.

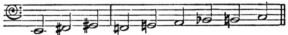

RESULT IN PLAYING.

Notes actually
  heard.

Thus we find that Peter Philips's "virginals" had a compass extending over three octaves and a sixth, *i.e.* from C under the bass staff to *A* above the treble staff, but altogether omitting the "black notes" C♯ D♯ F♯ and G♯ in the lowest octave. Hence the term "short" octave.

Short Octaves.

Such an arrangement of the notes of the lowest octave was quite common in church organs from 1500 to 1800 or later. There are even persons still living who remember the "short octave" as an actual fact of ecclesiastical musicianship. It was managed somewhat differently in more extended keyboards, *e.g.*, if the keyboard really had the visible semitones down to C [music], the organist was likely to find that

the apparent C sharp would produce A [music], a

much more useful note in the days of unequal temperament, and so on.

Peter Philips's pieces, Pavana Doloroso and Galiarda Doloroso (*en suite*), dated 1593, tell us very plainly of the short octave on his clavier. He ingeniously makes use of the peculiarity (which was quite common) by bringing in "long" chords, such as cannot be played by one hand nowadays, but which are perfectly easy under the "short-octave" system.

Instances are, i. 325, top line, 326, line 4, etc., 328, 329, all in the left-hand part, where Philips uses a whole series of chords including tenths, some of which at least are impossible now, unless played *arpeggiando*.

An example from the end of the Galiarda Doloroso (p. 329) will make the method quite clear.

TENTHS MADE EASY BY " SHORT OCTAVE."

PETER PHILIPS (dated 1593).

Here the left-hand part is rendered possible for the smallest hand by the tuning described above, for all the tenths simply become ordinary octave stretches, the player merely following his thumb with his little finger. (The tenth marked * would be less still, viz., F♯ F, a stretch of a major seventh.)

Philips uses the "short octave" elsewhere (i. 287, an arrangement of a madrigal) to make the left hand play a big chord of 4 notes, [musical notation], which of course is quite feasible, for the low G♯ key (see the explanation above, p. 151) has the low E on it, so all the player has to do is to strike [musical notation].

It is obvious that Philips was much struck with the value of this common peculiarity of the virginals of his time, indeed he uses it so frequently in the Pavan and Galliard above named as to lead one to believe that he wrote these two movements with the special purpose of showing how these large chords or intervals could be made available.

On the other hand, Bull and Tomkins appear to have possessed virginals of four clear octaves from

to   , with or without a short octave at the low end. I cannot clearly decide on the last point. The highest note in the whole book (unless I have missed some very rare case) is the treble *a* named above.

References to the use of the A beneath the bass staff are : *Bull*, i. 177, 179; ii. 22. *Tomkins*, ii. 56, 96, 102.

Bull, in ii. 22, has this chord   , which (with the other passages mentioned) makes it likely that he had *all* the semitones down to low A, on their proper keys.

ii. 56 shows on lines 2 and 6 that Tomkins had at least these notes in the lowest octave of his keyboard :—

LOWEST OCTAVE.

TOMKINS (Elizabethan).

An anonymous writer (ii. 312), in a short Alman (already quoted, p. 131), uses the following :—

ANONYMOUS "SHORT OCTAVE."

(Elizabethan or earlier.)

which would be possible on a keyboard with a short octave
ending with the C below the bass staff, having the low A
tuned on to the C♯ key, a common arrangement on the organs
of the 18th century and earlier.

These last two writers may therefore have used instruments like " Queen Elizabeth's Virginal " (South Kensington
Museum),* the keyboard of which possesses 5 keys below the

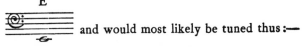 and would most likely be tuned thus :—

NAMES OF THE KEYS.

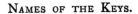

NOTES PRODUCED IN PLAYING

The top note of this clavier is high C,

Here must be mentioned a curious difficulty which arises in
considering Philips's pieces in connection with the " short
octave," which his instrument certainly had. Plainly, it is
this, that whereas the arrangement described on p. 151 provides only C D E F G A as the lowest notes which could
really be sounded by the player, nevertheless Philips uses the

low G♯ more than once in the Pavana Doloroso,

viz., i. 322 and 323, bottom lines.   The two cases are

* See Frontispiece.

properly only one, as the second is merely a repetition or variation of the first. Still it is a difficulty, and requires explanation.

The passage is as follows, in the simpler form of i. 322 :—

PETER PHILIPS (1593).

etc.

The G♯ in the bass, as before explained, had no place in the " short octave " scheme, upon which the rest of this piece is ordered. The first suggestion would naturally be that the sharp is simply a mistake. This is not impossible, for the passage is quite smooth and right without the sharp, as may be seen best by playing it over so, as far as the asterisk.

But this explanation is untenable—(a) because the G♯ is well defined two lines above, in a similar passage, and (b) because the MS. itself is perfectly clear about the sharp.

Another explanation might be found in the rather remarkable fact that there are 19 pieces by Philips in the Fitzwilliam Virginal Book, and that the note ⸬ is found nowhere in the whole 19, except in this one place. May we suppose, then, that Philips wrote the passage, including this apparently impossible note, knowing quite well that it was impossible, just as Beethoven or Schubert did in the case of their contrabasso parts ?

But a simpler explanation is still at our hand, which may solve the difficulty. It is quite likely that Philips's instrument had a " split " key on G♯, that is, a key made in halves, one part of which would play the low E (as already explained), and the other G♯. Double keys of this kind were fairly common in the old " short octave " claviers. Mersenne (1636) apparently speaks of a divided key below the C under the bass staff, the two halves of which sounded GG and FFF, the AA and BB being on CC♯ and DD♯, so that a complete scale of " white " notes was available down to

FFF

Additional evidence as to the practice of the middle 17th century is furnished by Mr A. J. Hipkins (Grove, IV. 305a, note), who speaks of split keys in short octaves, with date 1664.

Thus it is very probable that Peter Philips wrote his Pavana Doloroso (1593) for an instrument which had its low G♯ key " split," so as to provide for the note G♯ as well as the note E.

Finally, although the G♯ may have been a novelty (indeed, Italian instruments seem never to have provided for it when the lowest key was E), the short octave itself was none, for examples are to be had of this arrangement of the bass notes before 1500.

FINGERING IN THE SIXTEENTH CENTURY.

We have not yet reached the height of von Bülow's ideal, namely, that the correct fingering of a pianoforte piece is that which makes it possible to play the piece in any key without further cogitation on the part of the performer. On the contrary, there are still with us excellent persons who would hesitate to use the thumb on a black key, if there was any alternative.

This being so in the 20th century, let us be careful in

our judgment of a much earlier time, with its even more elementary notions, and a far less satisfactory instrument on which to exercise those notions.

A book was published at Leipzig in 1571, by a German called Ammerbach, entitled "Orgel oder Instrument Tablatur," which tells how the scales were fingered in his day. Mr W. H. Cummings ("Proceedings of the Musical Association," London, 1893, page 11) gives the important details of this scale fingering as follows :—

1. The right hand thumb was *not used at all.*
2. The little fingers very rarely employed.
3. When the thumb of the left hand was occasionally used, it was marked with a o.
4. The index finger was marked 1, and the others 2, 3, 4.

Thus we see that what is now called "English" fingering was "German" fingering in 1571. And this was still the case in 1697, when Daniel Speer published a book called "Das Musicalische Kleeblatt," which gives the same signs, o, 1, 2, 3, 4, and shows that the right thumb was still entirely neglected, although the left-hand thumb was more frequently used.

Various other books, including Mattheson's "Kleine Generalbassschule" (1735) and Maies's "Musiksaal" (1741), show that the o, 1, 2, 3, 4, was still used in Germany, and that the thumbs were generally unused, especially the thumb of the right hand.

An Italian book, "La prima albori musicali, etc.," by Father Lorenzo Penna, printed five times between 1656 and 1696, gives fingering allowing of the use of the three middle fingers only, and ignoring both the thumbs and both the little fingers.

While this sort of thing was going on on the Continent, we find that England always used the thumbs and little fingers quite freely, and marked the fingering with 1, 2, 3, 4, 5. This was so in 1599, the date of a MS. book of lessons for the virginals, fully fingered, and it was still so in 1757, the date of the last edition of " The Muses' Delight."

The system of naming the fingers +, 1, 2, 3, 4 seems to have been first brought to England by a German, Rudolph Falkener, who published "Instructions for playing the Harpsichord" in 1762 and 1774. Another German called Heck tried to counteract these evil ways, and to re-introduce the old English fingering, 1, 2, 3, 4, 5, speaking on his title-page of " such as have accustomed themselves to a wrong way of fingering." Heck did not succeed in his effort, and Clementi (who came to London in 1777), together with Dussek (who arrived in 1788), completed the fell work by setting up as music publishers and marking their fingering +,1, 2, 3, 4. Thus the original German fingering came to England, and has since been wrongly known as " English."

In the meantime the Germans had very sensibly adopted the English method, for Emmanuel Bach's " Versuche," the letterpress of which is dated 1759, uses 1, 2, 3, 4, 5, and fingers the scale of C in many various ways, including

and

And thus the " English " fingering has, ever since, been known as " German." For the sake of completeness it may be stated here that Couperin's " L'Art de toucher le

Clavecin " (Paris, 1717) marks the fingering in the English way, viz., 1, 2, 3, 4, 5.

A slight notion of the principal difference between modern pianoforte fingering and that of such men as Couperin and J. S. Bach may be got from these two passages, fingered by Couperin :—

RIGHT HAND.

'and

LEFT HAND.

In the first example, 3 is passed over 2. Emmanuel Bach, forty years later, disallowed this, but his father John Sebastian still practised it. Emmanuel also said that only the thumb might pass under. His father, however, allows even the little finger to pass under the third (*i.e.* 5 under 4).

John Sebastian Bach told his son Emmanuel that when he was young, the thumb was only used for great stretches. In this connection, it may be worth while pointing out that in the Fitzwilliam Virginal Book it is the rule for the big chords to be in the left-hand part; and this may have led to the habit of using the left-hand thumb more freely than that of the right hand, which seems to have been a long established custom in Germany, judging from the account of Ammerbach's fingering (1571), given above (p. 158).

The student cannot be too careful in keeping clearly before him that the essential difference between the modern pianoforte and the old " plectrum " claviers renders it misleading to judge of the ancient method of fingering from his knowledge of what is suitable on the keyed instruments of our own day.

In the first place, "touch," in our sense, could not exist on the virginals, spinet, or harpsichord (all of these were "plectrum" claviers), except with a limited meaning. A "smart" downward pressure, and an equally "smart" return of the finger in an upward direction was necessary, on account of the mechanism itself. What we call "evenness" of touch mattered not at all, again, on account of the "plectral" action. "Repetition" of one note, however rapid, was perhaps better done with *one* finger than with several.* Again we see the essential difficulty of judging the 16th or 17th century fingering, when the judge knows only the pianoforte, and that in its perfected form.

Again, a method, whether of "touch" or of mere fingering, suitable to the harpsichord class of keyed instrument, might well be unsuited to the clavichord, which had a "tangent" action and not a "plectral," and which, therefore, required both evenness and gentleness in the playing. Once more we perceive how misleading it may be to judge from the pianoforte to the older claviers. In this case (the German "tangent" clavier) we find an instrument possessing at any-rate two features which are not present either in the piano-forte or the harpsichord, viz., the possibility of inducing slight temporary alterations in the pitch of a note, by pressing it more or less strongly ; and the "Bebung," or *vibrato*, which could be got on a single note by rocking the finger on the key.

These facts must be remembered in studying the specimens of 16th century fingering which have come down to us in the Fitzwilliam Virginal Book.

It is fortunate that examples of Bull's fingering occur in this collection, for he probably represents the high-water

* This is the experience of modern players on the virginals. The Eliza-bethans themselves, however, seem to have thought differently ; see p. 164 below.

mark of 16th or early 17th century agility. But in addition to Bull, instances are found in pieces by Munday, Byrd, and others.

John Munday's " Fantasia" in the Æolian Mode (i. 19) is not very interesting musically, but will serve to introduce us to the "Fingering of the Sixteenth Century," as marked in the Fitzwilliam Book.

Munday's piece, above named, has this passage for the right hand on p. 19.

with fingering as marked.

I suppose that the complete fingering may have been

A similar passage in the next line for the *left* hand is marked with a 3 on the corresponding note, and thus was most likely fingered 3 2 1, 3 2 1, 3 2 1, just as we should do it now, with the thumb on the first quaver of each beat.

The same composer's " Fantasia on the Weather," i. 23, has a suggestion that Munday used the five-finger exercise as we do:—

The fingering given in the MS. is merely the 3 in bar 2. It seems clear that the fingering printed above the notes is implied, therefore John Munday probably used 1, 2, 3, 4, 5 in order over five adjacent notes, and understood the " contraction " of the hand implied in the change from 5 to 3 on the same note, and accepted the most modern dictum that similar passages should have similar fingering if possible. In the same piece (p. 26) we find the following for right hand,

The 5, 4, 3 underneath is given in the MS., and I presume it to imply what is printed above the notes.

Bull has an interesting line (i. 70) in a Galiarda, which seems to show that he too thought it well that passages of a similar outline should have the same fingering; and, at the same time, tends to prove that he avoided the thumb except for chord playing.

As in MS.—

BULL'S FINGERING.

JOHN BULL (1563-1628.)

The continual recurrence of 5, 2 is instructive. The note marked with the asterisk is a difficulty. If correct, it must mean that the note before, e, was intended to be played by 2, and not by 1, which one would certainly have expected. It

seems likely to be a mistake, for the result of having 3 on F♯ prevents 5 being on the following B, and breaks the clear rule of the whole passage.

(*N.B.*—The treble part of line 4, bar 1, on p. 71, is plainly incorrect, and should read—

as is seen by comparing line 1, bar 3, of p. 71.)

An unknown author provides another puzzle, reflecting the want of certainty in the use of the thumb, in a Præludium, i. 82, lines 2 and 3, where the *change of fingers* for repeated notes is marked with a thoroughness which is quite of our own time, but the thumb apparently avoided, as a rule, in spite of its obvious value.

FINGERING (UNCERTAIN AUTHOR), FITZWILLIAM BOOK, i. 82.

Some of this is quite in the modern style. But it is hard to see why the thumb should have been disregarded in the three cases underlined, where 2, 2 is used, although every consideration would have indicated 2, 1 as the right fingering.

Bull seems to have believed entirely in changing fingers for rapid repetition of the same note, *e.g.*, in his Pavana, i. 125.

BULL'S FINGERING.

Right Hand.

A passage on the previous page (i. 124) illustrates other probable features of his system :—

Right Hand.

Bull's own fingering is *under* the notes : my guess at the rest of it is given above.

On the next page of the same piece (i. 126) is a passage showing Bull apparently avoiding the right-hand thumb, but using that of the left hand freely.

VARIATION ON STRAIN 2 OF PAVANA, WITH FINGERING AS IN MS.

JOHN BULL.

The use of the left-hand thumb in the short ascending passages in bar 1 is quite plain, as is the avoidance of the right-hand thumb in bars 3 and 4.

On p. 128 there is evidence that Bull was uncertain in his use of the figures for the left hand, and that he, with others (such as Byrd and G. Farnaby), sometimes used 1 for the little finger, and 5 for the thumb of the left hand, *e.g.*,

which can only mean what I have put *over* the notes. Bull's fingering (as usual) I have put underneath.

Other singular instances of the fingering of this piece must be passed over.

Byrd, in a Præludium (i. 83, line 1, and i. 84, line 4), shows that 5 meant " thumb " in the left hand; and similarly Giles Farnaby, in the second line of " The King's Hunt," i. 196. An interesting feature of the latter case is the ornament interpreted by Mr Dannreuther as a " slide." The fingering curiously confirms the interpretation, while the interpretation naturally explains the fingering, which would otherwise have been inexplicable. The bar runs thus :—

FINGERING AS IN MS.

GILES FARNABY.

Left hand—

meaning this—

A similar " slide " appears in the right-hand part of the same bar, fingered in a more comprehensible manner, *i.e.*

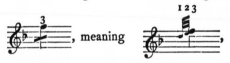

, meaning

Byrd seems to have the crossing of 4 over 5, *e.g.*, 4545 ascending.

FITZWILLIAM BOOK, i. 84.

BYRD (1538-1623).

R. H.
L. H.

which I take to mean something like the following :—

R. H.

This is from a Præludium (printed also in "Parthenia" as Prelude to the "Carman's Whistle"), the reference in the Fitzwilliam Book being i. 84.

The reader now has before him most of the typical specimens of 16th century fingering contained in the Fitzwilliam Virginal Book.

We gather from them: (1) That the English writers of the Elizabethan time used 1, 2, 3, 4, 5 to denote the fingers of each hand, but that there were various uncertainties, *e.g.*, some composers used 1 for the little finger of the left hand, and 5 for the thumb. (This was also the arrangement contained in a "Collection of Ayres," published in London in 1700.)

(2) That the use of the right-hand thumb was avoided, but by no means forbidden. (This apparently was still the case under Mattheson in 1735 and Maies in 1741.)

(3) That the fingering of scale passages was uncertain, and generally based on the crossing of fingers, rather than on the "passing" of the thumb.

(This also appears to have gone on until the time of Emmanuel Bach, *i.e.* the middle 18th century.)

(4) Rapid repetition was practised with change of fingers.

With regard to this last, the student must be warned again that repetition on a harpsichord is not in the least like repetition on a pianoforte.

CHAPTER XIV

ORGAN PIECES, PRELUDES, MADRIGALS (TRANSCRIPTIONS)

THERE still remain three classes of pieces in the Fitzwilliam Book which have not been reviewed in these chapters, viz., the 17 " Organ " pieces (settings of ecclesiastical melodies, etc.) ; the 19 Preludes (13 by six writers, and 6 more anonymous) ; and Philips's arrangements of 9 Italian Madrigals or parts of Madrigals, with which may be included Giles Farnaby's own arrangement of his Canzonet, " Ay me, poor heart " (ii. 330, followed by another movement, ii. 333), and Bull's variations on Dowland's Madrigal, " If my complaint " (ii. 242 and 244), which was published in 1597 as one of Dowland's First Set of Songs, and as " Captain Piper's Galliard " in his " Lachrymæ," 1605.

ORGAN PIECES.

The class first named, which seems on the whole to be referable to the organ, consists mainly of 13 pieces founded on Church Melodies, and comprises examples by Tallis, Bull, Parsons, Byrd, Blitheman, and an anonymous writer.

These pieces are amongst the earliest examples of the method of embroidering an Ecclesiastical hymn tune with a contrapuntal accompaniment, which was practised in the 16th century by Netherlanders (Sweelinck), Italians (the two Gabriellis, of Venice), and by various Englishmen. Relics of the practice are to be found in J. S. Bach's organ works more than a century later.

They are naturally founded on the general method of the

mediæval vocal part music, where a Church Melody was taken as a basis (known as Canto Fermo) for an extended movement or movements, *e.g.*, the Mass.

Naturally, also, they are altogether " Modal " in character, and are further from modernity than any of the dances or other pieces which are in this collection.

As a rule, these "organ" pieces will be found without interest to the modern mind ; but much may be gathered by a careful study of their main features. *Anon.* (i. 421) supplies us with an example of the simplest way of doing these things, namely, the plain song in the right hand, and a continuous " run " in the left hand, thus :—

" VENI."

ANON (date ? 1550).

Here the running counterpoint defines the implied harmony conveniently for us moderns, who have generally lost the tradition, *e.g.*—

THE SAME, PLAIN.

This, of course, is got by taking the principal notes of the " run " as the bass, and occasionally a hint from the same source concerning the precise form of the chord indicated by the bass.

The progression of the two first chords given above would probably be fatal in a modern " examination "; however, it was not avoided in the 16th century, in spite of the " tritone " contained therein (*i.e.* the augmented 4th, with the B in the one chord, the F in the other). It may be seen again, quite clearly implied, on p. 422, bars 4 and 5, where the tritone occurs in its most plain-spoken shape, in the extreme parts, viz., the treble and bass. I now give the whole of this Plain Song, with the harmonies implied by this anonymous 16th century composer.

" VENI " (FITZWILLIAM BOOK, i. 421).

Harmonies taken from the counterpoint of ANON. 1550?

p. 422.

E.W.N.

The final pause chord is given as in the original. The rest of the "reduction" probably does not much misrepresent the implied harmonies of the Fitzwilliam author. The "flat" seventh note of the Æolian mode is well shown in the 3rd bar from the end, where the harmony indicated by the counterpoint of the original piece absolutely prevents the G from being anything but "natural." Also the tritone, as already stated, is to be seen more than once, undisguised and apparently without blame. The same Canto Fermo is set by Bull (i. 138); a short extract is given above, p. 76.

Two works of this kind, by Thomas Tallis, both entitled "Felix namque," are given. The first (i. 427) is the earliest dated piece in the book, 1562; the second (ii. 1) is dated 1564. A specimen of the former will be sufficient to give an idea of both. I select passages where the plainsong happens to repeat itself more or less, so that the composer may be seen treating the same notes in two ways, viz.—

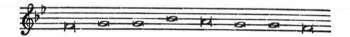

PART OF "FELIX NAMQUE"

(FITZWILLIAM BOOK, i. 429, l. 5).

THOMAS TALLIS (dated 1562).

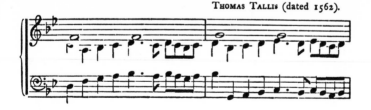

The chromatic harmony (bars 5 and 6) is worth noticing. The chord marked * really has the previous minim "g" sustained over it, and should be compared with the asterisked chord in the next extract.

The same notes as set on p. 431, l. 1.

THOMAS TALLIS (dated 1562).

The chord marked * is very strange. Also I suspect the
final crotchet (marked †) in the left hand of the bar before
should be D F, instead of E G.

Several examples are by Bull. "Christe Redemptor"
(ii. 64) has the Canto Fermo in the tenor, with treble and
bass counterpoint added, in continual imitation. It is dry,
which is a pity, for the plain song is a fine one, and I give
it here as Bull has it, omitting the repetition of notes less
than breves.

"CHRISTE REDEMPTOR" AS GIVEN BY BULL

(FITZWILLIAM BOOK, ii. 64).

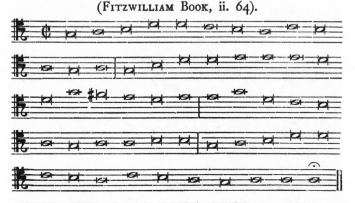

A very short quotation will be sufficient to show the
aridity of Bull's treatment.

"CHRISTE REDEMPTOR."

JOHN BULL.

C.F. in TENOR, one note in each bar.

This plainsong is known elsewhere as "Jesu dulcis memoria," and may be seen in "Hymns Ancient and Modern" (No. 177), fitted with harmonies which in many instances can only be regarded as out of place.

The plain song "Gloria Tibi Trinitas" is set no less than five times in this series of pieces, three settings being by Bull, the others by Parsons (Robert the father, who died 1570, or John his son) and William Blitheman, who is said to have been Bull's master. In four out of the five cases the piece is called

"In nomine"

which may perhaps be explained by the dialect of North-East Yorkshire, where, till recent times, it was not uncommon to speak of any set of verses as a "nomminy," with a reference to words such as had to be committed to memory. This title, "In nomine," may therefore merely mean "Hymn."

Blitheman's effort (mostly in 3 parts) is dry (i. 181). Some patience is required to find the notes of the plainsong in Parsons' setting (ii. 135), which is somewhat confused, and mostly in four parts.

Two of John Bull's settings (i. 135 and i. 160) of this hymn are not very exhilarating, but the remaining one (ii. 34) requires some notice, partly because of its greater musical value, partly because it is a characteristic example of Bull's fondness for experiment. In this case the whole piece (six heavy pages) is in $\frac{11}{4}$ time. The final page is further complicated by the dotting of the notes, and the last bar but one on p. 39 (being part only of one of the $\frac{11}{4}$ bars, printed so for convenience of reading) contains the puzzling combination of 9 quavers (R. H.), a minim and two crotchets (tenor), and a dotted minim and dotted crotchet (bass).

The rhythmical experiment, however, is not without success, and a specimen of the first few bars is now given. The Canto Fermo is in the bass.

First Notes of "Gloria Tibi Trinitas."

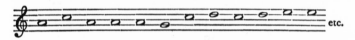

First Bars of Bull's Setting (Fitzwilliam Book, ii. 34).

Canto Fermo in the Bass (each note 11 beats).

Plain Song in Bass, one note in each bar.

Bull's liking for complications may be illustrated from the "Gloria Tibi Trinitas," found in i. 160, where on p. 162, lines 2 and 3, the bass and alto exhibit the "Proportion" known as "Sesquialtera," *i.e.* 2 equal notes against 3 of the same.

EXTRACT FROM ANOTHER SETTING OF "*GLORIA TIBI TRINITAS*," SHOWING "PROPORTION" OF "SESQUIAL-TERA" (3 to 2).

(Canto Fermo in the treble. One note to each bar.)

Dr BULL.

Another well-worn plainsong is set by Bull under the name of "Salvator Mundi" (i. 163).

This is very generally set to "Come, Holy Ghost" (Veni, Creator) in English hymn-books.

Bull produces three variations, with the Canto Fermo in the treble. The first variation is in two parts, the left-hand part consisting mainly of runs. An interesting extract, however, is the following :—

EXAMPLE OF ARPEGGIOS AND BROKEN CHORDS
(FITZWILLIAM BOOK, i. 163).

(From near the end of line 2 of plainsong "Salvator Mundi," or "Come, Holy Ghost.")   BULL, 1563-1628.

The sturdy harmonies of the following (i. 166) portion of the 2nd variation are worth considering. (I begin the extract where the plainsong joins on to the corresponding E which ends the above quotation from variation 1.)

FROM THE SAME. VARIATION 2. (FITZWILLIAM BOOK, i. 166.)

BULL.

I have purposely simplified the bass here, in order that the reader's attention may be fixed on the *musical* interest of the passage. As a matter of *technical* interest, it may now be mentioned that the bass is in the form of broken octaves, ornamented by mordents—thus—

etc.

After ten bars like this, the form of the bass becomes even more complicated.

THE SAME, i. 167.

Here, in the first bar, the four crotchets in the right-hand part denote that Dr Bull suddenly forgot how slow the Canto Fermo was, and managed to have four notes of it in one bar. Consequently he had to pull up quickly, and do the three notes C A G over again at the proper pace, in the next three bars.

It may be of value to point out, that although Bull harmonises this plainsong sometimes with F♮, sometimes with F♯, e.g., the opening notes—

Harmony Implied, i. 163, l. 1.

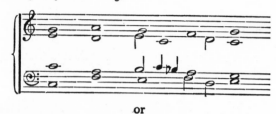

or

From i. 167, l. 5.

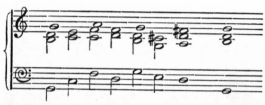

he shows no sign of altering a somewhat critical B♮ near the end of the plainsong, hampered as it is by an F, which to more modern ears would present a difficulty in harmonisation.

The Same, i. 164.
(Implied Harmonies, end of var. 1.)

Bull.

The harmonies given by Bull in the second and third variations at this point, make B♭ altogether impossible.

On the other hand, Bull's setting of " Gloria Tibi Trinitas " (i. 137, l. 4) introduces an altered note in the plainsong which is not found in the other four settings of that melody mentioned above, two of which are by Bull himself, and the others by Blitheman and Parsons. The phrase (Æolian, "transposed," *i.e.* with *one flat* in the signature, the pitch being lowered a perfect fifth) is as follows :—

LAST PHRASE OF " GLORIA TIBI TRINITAS " (TRANSPOSED).
Harmonies implied by Blitheman, i. 182, l. 4.

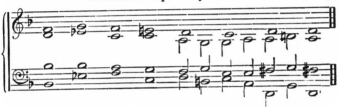

Bull's harmonies are not widely different from this, but he alters the E♮ to E♭, thus—

LAST PHRASE OF " GLORIA TIBI TRINITAS," WITH BULL'S CHORDS AND ALTERED E (FITZWILLIAM BOOK, i. 137).

These harmonies are merely simplified from the original florid passages (i. 137), and are well worth study, as is the whole treatment of the last six bars of this piece.

Lastly, in Bull's setting, i. 160, quoted from above (p. 180), another alteration is allowed, viz., the last note but one (*e.g.*, in the last extract the note C) is sharpened (i. 162).

Alterations of this kind are always to be found in music of the period, and the practice seems to depend entirely on convenience. The same remark applies to similar cases in J. S. Bach's Choral Preludes on well-known hymns, and to his use of the Canto Fermo in his Church Cantatas, where the actual tones and semitones of the plainsong are not allowed to interfere with Bach's added vocal and instrumental parts.

Three pieces of this class, called " Miserere," are included in the MS. The one by Bull, ii. 442, with three variations on the plainsong, in 3 parts, is very dry indeed.

The other two are by Byrd, and are worked on a different melody from that given by Bull. The setting with the melody in the alto (ii. 232) is in four parts, and has already been referred to (p. 74 and following) and quoted from as a possible example of "tonal" answer in fugue. A rather important correction of ii. 233, l. 3, in this piece has also been given in the same place. The arrangement in three parts by Byrd is in ii. 230, but is not interesting enough to deserve an extract.

" Heaven and Earth " (i. 415) probably belongs to this group of ecclesiastical pieces, as it seems to be written round some plainsong or another. The author *may* be Mr Tregian, but this is doubtful. Musically, the piece is without value. The words may have something to do with the " Sanctus " or " Te Deum."

Four pieces called " Grounde " may be considered here. They are, of course, variations on " ground bass," and therefore somewhat related to the exercises on Canto Fermo which have just been dealt with. Giles Farnaby's "Groũde" (ii. 353) consists of 14 variations, some of them very difficult, on the following "grounde."

FITZWILLIAM BOOK, ii. 353.

GILES FARNABY (16th century).

etc.

I give this mainly as a good example of the absolute want of "key" feeling in the "grounde" itself, which may be useful to the student of these matters (see above, p. 138 ff.). But it will also serve as an instance of the use of "bars" in these early days, e.g., the "grounde" is apparently in triple time, whereas the piece immediately proceeds (at the entrance of the tenor part) in duple or quadruple time. Again, the student will observe that the sign ₵ does not refer to the probable contents of any bar, but simply and solely to the relative values of notes occurring in any bar, e.g., that a semibreve contains *two* minims, and not three.*

* The following cases, gathered from the Fitzwilliam Book, will be of interest to students :—

Sign used in MS.	Modern Meaning.	Reference.
C	$\frac{3}{2}$	i. 267
₵	$\frac{4}{4}$	ii. 453
₵	$\frac{6}{4}$ and $\frac{4}{4}$	ii. 489
₵	$\frac{4}{2}$	ii. 51
₵	$\frac{6}{2}$	ii. 450
₵	$\frac{6}{4}$ or $\frac{6}{2}$ or $\frac{6}{4}$	i. 218, i. 54, i. 421
3	$\frac{3}{2}$	ii. 486
3	$\frac{3}{4}$	ii. 471

and the one just given, where ₵ is used indifferently for either 3 or 2 semibreves in the "bar."

Thus, to take one example, the sign ₵ may mean either $\frac{6}{4}$, $\frac{4}{2}$, $\frac{4}{4}$, $\frac{6}{4}$; or, $\frac{3}{2}$ may be expressed by 3, ₵, ₵, or C.

Byrd's variations on "Tregian's Ground" (probably not Tregian's but Hugh Ashton's, see the Nevell book) are good music (i. 226), but are better classed with the variations on Dances, as the ground is practically a Galliard. William Inglott's "Galliard Ground" (ii. 375) is dry. Much the best of these pieces is Thomas Tomkins's (ii. 87) "A Grounde." The variations are interesting, and are founded on a very short but quaint subject—which seems to be taken from the popular tune called "Up Tails All," set by Giles Farnaby (ii. 360).

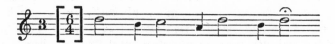

Here are short examples of the many ways in which Tomkins uses this little subject :—

THOMAS TOMKINS (16th century).

In the bass.

In the treble.

In the treble.

In Canon.

etc.

PRELUDES.

There are nineteen "Preludes" in the Fitzwilliam Book, six by anonymous writers, seven by Dr Bull, two by Byrd, and the rest by Galeazzo (an unknown person), Sweelinck, Giles Farnaby, and Thomas Oldfield (another unknown). As a class, these Preludes are not interesting, as they generally consist of chords ornamented by florid passages, runs, shakes, and arpeggios, which were merely meant to warm the player's fingers before embarking on a more serious performance.

Few of them can be regarded as part of a "suite" of pieces. Amongst those which are so, however, we find the two by Byrd; i. 83, which is known (from "Parthenia") to be the Prelude to "The Carman's Whistle," and i. 394, which is *en suite* with the Fantasia in i. 188.

Bull's Prelude in the Dorian mode (i. 158) is said (by Ward) to be the "Prelude to Gloria Tibi Trinitas." If this is the case, the particular setting of that plainsong which it belongs to may be the one in i. 135, and not the one which immediately follows it in the volume (i. 160). There is, however, nothing in common between the melody of "Gloria Tibi Trinitas" and the music of this particular Prelude.

Bull's Preludes are mainly valuable as supplying specimens of the high technical standard which he must have attained. Among such are the following :—

TECHNICAL PASSAGES FROM BULL'S PRELUDES

I. (FITZWILLIAM BOOK, i. 419—Mixolydian.)

Right hand   BULL.

etc.

2. (Fitzwilliam Book, ii. 260—Mixolydian.)

BULL.

3. (Fitzwilliam Book, ii. 274—Æolian.)

BULL.

etc.

From these three sample passages we have (*a*) rapid repetition in both hands, (*b*) chord passages for right hand, (*c*) broken octaves and other broken intervals, (*d*) extended scales, in both hands, and in contrary motion, and in similar motion at the interval of a sixth.

An example of arpeggio has already been quoted. See above, p. 181.

Giles Farnaby's Prelude in the Ionian Mode (ii. 372) is worth naming with Bull's efforts, for it is really difficult, and only a thoroughly neat player could do it well.

The example by Sweelinck (i. 378) is hardly in the same class with the others, for it is called "Preludium Toccata," and is far more a " Fantasia " than a Prelude, being fugal in character and six pages in length. Amongst other difficulties, it contains the following for left hand :—

FITZWILLIAM BOOK, i. 383.

Left hand   J. P. SWEELINCK.

The Anonymous Preludes (six in number) are more sensible than any of the others, especially the Ionian one at i. 85, and the Æolian at ii. 169, which latter piece has some real musical interest over and above the scales and runs in which it abounds (*e.g.*, one passage in semiquavers, for the left hand, goes on for fourteen bars). An extract has already been given from the Prelude at i. 81, showing some curious fingering of a difficult passage (see above, p. 164).

MADRIGALS.

It is not necessary to say much about the transcriptions of Madrigals which are given in the Fitzwilliam Book. They are not really of any great importance. The method of "arrangement" is what might be expected, viz., the plain harmonies of the original vocal parts are used by the transcriber as a skeleton on which to hang elaborate passages, shakes, runs, and other ornaments. A few bars illustrating this method are given in the "Oxford History of Music," vol. iii. p. 94, where an extract from Philips's arrangement of *Cosi morirò* (by Luca Marenzio) is printed, with the corresponding bars of the original.

The same work (vol. iii. p. 42) quotes a passage from Caccini's Madrigal (so named) for solo voice and accompaniment, "Amarilli, mia bella," an arrangement of which appears in the Fitzwilliam Virginal Book, by Peter Philips, dated 1603. Here is Caccini's original, with Philips's transcription printed immediately below it.

"AMARILLI, MIA BELLA" for solo voice and accompaniment, by Caccini (Julio Romano), 1558-1640.

A - ma-ril-li, mia bel-la, non cre-di del mio cor dol - - ce de si ro etc.

The same, transcribed for the Virginals by Peter Philips, dated 1603.

FITZWILLIAM BOOK, i. 329.

The lengthening of the original Caccini by Philips may point to the method of singing the madrigal, *e.g.*, the slight pause after " bella," which he fills up with a run ; and the extension of the second syllable in " desiro," which may well represent some singer's trick lingering in Philips's memory from an actual performance of the piece.

The following short extract is not without interest :—

" TIRSI " (the " first part " of a madrigal in three movements, " FRENO " and " COSI MORIRO " being the other two. From " Musica Transalpina," published in London, 1588).

LUCA MARENZIO (1550-1599).

Peter Philips transcribes the passage thus :—

FITZWILLIAM BOOK, i. 280.

The same arranged by PHILIPS.

etc.

Philips's fifth bar is a rather clever attempt to render the difficulty presented in the Soprano and Alto at the words "dye desired," where the two voices cross and the melody consequently is hidden. The largeness of effect produced by the full vocal harmony at the repetition of the word "Thirsis" is indicated by the florid passage in Philips's 7th bar.

Besides the 9 arrangements of madrigal movements by Peter Philips, there may be included in this class of pieces

Giles Farnaby's own transcription of his Canzonet " Ay me, poore heart " * (ii. 330, 333), and Bull's Galliard called (Captain) Piper's Galliard (ii. 242), which is a well-known madrigal by Dowland, and is found in Dowland's " First Set of Songs " (1597), set to the words " If my complaint could passion move."

* Date 1598.

CHAPTER XV

THE following paragraphs, in the shape of notes on about 30 of the composers represented in the Fitzwilliam Book, are intended as a practical guide to the student who wishes to examine the printed edition for himself. Out of such a mass of music (nearly 1000 folio pages) it is difficult to extract that which is most valuable, unless much time is available for the purpose.

It may be really useful, then, to indicate shortly the pieces which appear to deserve attention in the first place.

1. *Bull* (said to be a pupil of Blitheman, see above, p. 185) stands almost in a class by himself, as the Liszt of the 16th century. He was a real virtuoso. There is scarcely one, of over 40 pieces by him in this book, that does not show Bull in this light. He is not a man of sentiment, and thus stands in contrast with Byrd, Farnaby (Giles), and others of the Anonymous composers.

i. 70 is a good Galliard (see above, p. 164, for correction). "Dr Bull's Juell," ii. 128, is good. The "Spanish Pavan," ii. 131, is a capital tune and somewhat unusual. "The King's Hunt," ii. 116, is worth attention, especially the French Horn imitations. Another interesting piece is "The Duke of Brunswick's Alman," ii. 146.

2. *Byrd*. There are more than 70 pieces by Byrd, and most of them show signs of the Romantic spirit which is mainly absent from Bull's compositions. Although Byrd's

pieces are sometimes difficult, they are never so difficult as those of Bull, and apparently are never made difficult on purpose.

The Pavana, ii. 384, is beautiful. " The Mayden's Song," ii. 67, is quaint, and the first page or so is worth playing.* " Walsingham," i. 267, and " The woods so wilde," i. 263, are excellent. " John, come kisse me now," i. 47, is capital, also " Callino Casturame" (Colleen Oge Asthore), ii. 186. A pleasant " suite" may be made of " The Lavolta," ii. 180, " The Alman," ii. 182, and " Wolsey's Wilde," ii. 184. Finally, see i. 223, where, in his " Hunt's Up," Byrd has used the old catch " Now God be with old Simeon," at sec. 9, in wrong rhythm. (The same tune may be seen in ii. 435, in Byrd's "Pescodd Time," which is apparently another version of the " Hunt's Up.")

3. *Giles Farnaby* is as interesting as any composer in the whole collection. More than 50 pieces by him are included, and from them it may be gathered that he was a more clever player than Byrd, though nowhere near Bull in this respect. In sentiment and musical feeling Giles Farnaby's music is comparable with Byrd's.

The Galiarda, ii. 419, is of the very best, especially the antiphonal passages for the two hands on p. 420.

" Rosasolis," ii. 148, " Up Tails All," ii. 360, " Tower Hill," ii. 371 (short), and " Pawles Wharfe," ii. 17 (see above, p. 134), are worth playing.

" Put up thy dagger, Jemy," ii. 72, is a very good tune, and variations 1, 2, 3, 5 are of some interest.

The Duet for Two Virginals, i. 202, should not be overlooked, as a curiosity.

" Woody Cock," ii. 138, has a characteristic melody ; and

---

* Lilly's " Ancient Ballads and Broadsides " (1867) gives a 16th-century Ballad, " The Marchant's daughter of Bristow," " To the tune of The Mayden's Joy." Perhaps this " Mayden's Song " is the same.

pp. 143, 144 show a rather unusual "augmentation" of the second half of the tune.

"Quodling's Delight," ii. 19, is also very good, and may be usefully compared with a well-known and beautiful piece by Rameau (1683-1764), viz., the Gavotte and 6 variations in A minor. Quoted above, p. 135.

Also compare "Fain would I wed," ii. 263, by Richard Farnaby (the son).

4. *Anonymous* composers supply over 40 pieces, some of which are among the very best in the book.

Examples are: "Barafostus' Dream," i. 72 (see above, p. 83), the "Irishe Hohoane" (Ochone), i. 87, see plate facing p. 8; the Alman and Muscadin, i. 75 and 74; the Alman, i. 65; the Galliard, i. 77; and the King's Morisco, ii. 373.

5. *Thomas Morley.*—The author of one of the most sensible works ever written on Counterpoint and the rest of the subjects usually called "theoretical" (*lucus a non lucendo*, probably, such things being entirely "practical"). Morley's "Plain and Easy Introduction, etc." (1597) would entitle him to our respect, even if his compositions did not compel our admiration. But as a composer he is more than respectable. Some of his Madrigals are well known, and are among the best of their kind. His 9 pieces in the Fitzwilliam Book, though not showing him at his best, are good work, especially the Dances here named.

We may suppose a "Suite" in the three pieces—(*a*) Alman, ii. 171; (*b*) Pavana, ii. 173; (*c*) Galiarda, ii. 177.

(*a*) is in the Ionian Mode, (*b*) is Æolian, and is Dowland's celebrated "Lachrymæ." Also "set" by Byrd, ii. 42, and G. Farnaby, ii. 472. (*c*) The Galliard partly fulfils the old condition of using the melody of the preceding Pavana. (The same holds good of the Pavan and Galliard by Morley at ii. 209 and 213.)

ii. 177, line 3, bar 2, may be compared with Bach's Corantos, in respect of the uncertain rhythm (? $\frac{3}{2}$ *or* $\frac{6}{4}$) in the final bars of sections (Suites Anglaises, and some Partitas).

6. *Orlando Gibbons.* A great name. It is strange, the book contains only 2 pieces by Gibbons. Both, however, are more than worth hearing : the Pavana, ii. 479 (also found in Parthenia, 1611), and the setting of " The woods so wilde," i. 144, of which the most attractive portions are those numbered 1, 4, 6, 7, 8. These are specimens of the best quality of the Elizabethan school.

7. *Thomas Tomkins.* By whom are 5 pieces ; one, a setting of " Barafostus' Dreame," ii. 94, which is creditable, but not Romantic, as is the arrangement of *Anon.* at i. 72. The " Hunting Galliard," ii. 100, has a reminder of the melody of " Barafostus' Dreame" which immediately precedes it. It is worth playing up to line 2 of p. 101. Tomkins's " Grounde," ii. 87, is of some interest. It has already been described above, p. 188. Generally, the parts without " runs" are worth playing.

The Pavana, ii. 51, is very good indeed, and the portions without *agrémens* on pp. 51, 52, 54, are well worth playing for their harmonies. See above, p. 16, where it is quoted in its plainest form.

" Worster Braules," ii. 269, has a capital tune and good variations.

8. *John Munday* provides 5 pieces. " Munday's Joy," ii. 449, short and quaint ; * " Bonny sweet Robin," i. 66 (Hamlet ; and see above, p. 88), set also by G. Farnaby, ii. 77, whose work is altogether better stuff, see ii. 77, 78,† 80 (line 2). The first page of Munday's may be played.

---

* In bar 2 the minim in R. H. should be B G♯, and the quaver F preceding it in the alto will require a sharp.

† I suggest that on p. 78, l. 2, bar 3, the quaver rest in L. H. should be omitted as a mistake. The tenor E D may then be quavers, as in the MS.

"Goe from my window," i. 153, is uncertain, as it is almost the same as i. 42, where Thomas Morley is said to be the author. The Fantasia on the Weather, i. 23, is rubbish.* But see above, pp. 162, 163, concerning "fingering."

9. *Martin Peerson* (or Pierson). By whom are 4 pieces, not the worst in the book by any means : i. 359, "Alman," an excellent tune, and sensible variation; ii. 238, "Piper's Pavan" (Captain Piper). See Bull, ii. 242, for "Piper's *Galliard*," which, however, has nothing in common, and is a transcription of Dowland's familiar madrigal, "If my complaint could passion move."

"The Fall of the Leafe," ii. 423, and "The Primerose," ii. 422, have pretty tunes, and are worth hearing. These two little pieces of Peerson are in excellent company, as some particularly good short dances, etc., are to be found from ii. 412 to 421, as follows :—

(*a*) The Duchesse of Brunswick's Toye (*Bull*), ii. 412.

(*b*) A Toye (*Anon.*), ii. 413.

(*c*) Three Corantos (*Anon.*), ii. 414, 415.

(*d*) A first-rate and very difficult "Gigge" (*G. Farnaby*), ii. 416 (see above, p. 45).

(*e*) A Toye (*Anon.*), ii. 418.

(*f*) Galiarda; a beautiful tune (*G. Farnaby*), ii. 419.

(*g*) A Toye; see likeness to Bull's p. 412 (*G. Farnaby*), ii. 421.

10. *Robert Johnson.* Four pieces (2 arranged by Farnaby). Two Almans, one in the Dorian Mode, ii. 158; the other, ii. 159, certainly *not* so. For the latter, see above, pp. 137, 138. A beautiful Pavan (set, however, by G. Farnaby) is that at i. 141.†

---

* The first note should be A, not G.

† In R. Johnson's Pavan, i. 141, l. 4, bar 1, the final crotchet G in L. H. should be omitted ; and in the next bar the hypothetical crotchet rest should be replaced by the crotchet C, which follows it in the tenor part.

11. *William Inglott*. Born 1554. Organist of Hereford and Norwich. Died 1621, and is buried in Norwich Cathedral: ii. 375, a long " Ground " in Galliard time; ii. 381, variations on " The Leaves be greene; " tune mostly in bass or tenor; see var. 11, p. 383, l. 2, bar 2, where a semibreve, A, is missing in the Alto. Good work; better than some of the more pretentiously difficult pieces.

12. *Peter Philips*. Besides his 9 Madrigal movements, 8 of which are arranged from the work of four Italian composers, there are in the Fitzwilliam Virginal Book 10 original pieces by Philips; two Fantasias (Mixolydian, i. 335;* Ionian, i. 352); two Galliards (Mixolydian, i. 351; Dorian, doubly transposed, i. 296). The Mixolydian one is remarkable in its rhythm. The Pavana and Galiarda "Dolorosa" (? Tregian), dated 1593, i. 321 and 327, are particularly good, played "plain." The Galiarda is truly *one* with the Pavana. With the exception of section 1, the "Pavana Pagget (? Paget)," i. 291, is dull.

The "Passamezzo" Pavan and Galliard, i. 299 (date 1592) and i. 306 (with Saltarello at end of Galliard), are good and worth playing.

The Mixolydian Pavana, i. 343, is dated 1580, and is noted as " The first one Philips made."

The interesting connection of the Pavana and Galiarda "Dolorosa" with the mysteries of " short octaves," has already been fully dealt with above, see p. 153, etc.

13. *J. P. Sweelinck* (of Amsterdam). 4 pieces.

(*a*) Præludium Toccata, i. 378. A good example and worth playing through. More a Ricercar in places than a Toccata. See lines 1 and 2, contrary motion of answers in imitation. Vigorous passages for L. H., p. 382 and

* See ii. 406, Byrd's Fantasia, on the same subject.

(specially) 383 (see above, p. 192). See also L. H. passages, ii. 153, lines 1, 2, 3.

(*b*) Fantasia, ii. 297 (Dorian transposed). Contrary motion of answer again, in all four parts, during the whole piece. The "augmented" subject will be found pp. 298, 299 (contrary motion in Bass, line 4), and in "Tenor," p. 300, line 3, last semibreve. Once more in original shape on p. 303, line 4, tenor, on a Pedal in the Treble part. A good piece, worth playing.

(*c*) Psalme [140], ii. 151. Five variations on the Plain Song, in 2, 3, and (at end) 4 parts. Rather dry, but not so dry as Tallis and Bull in this kind. Line 1, etc., notice J. S. Bach's trick, of making the Counter Subject out of the Canto Fermo, already in full work, *e.g.* :—

J. P. SWEELINCK.

Also, the 4th variation contains the subject in diminution (treble), imitated by the tenor in augmentation.

(*d*) Ut, re, mi, fa, sol, la; ii. 26, in 4 parts, dated 1612. Fully described elsewhere, see p. 107, etc.

The various spellings of Sweelinck's name are somewhat comical. In (*a*) he is described as "Jehan Pieterson Swellinck"; in (*b*) the form changes to "Jhon Pieterson Sweeling," "Organista a Amstelreda"; in (*c*) we have "Jehan Pietersō Swelling"; and in (*d*) the "Pieterson" is spelt "Peterson."

Thus the accepted spelling "Sweelinck" does not appear in the Fitzwilliam Book.

14. *Thomas Warrock* (organist of Hereford, 1586). A Pavan and Galliard, i. 384, 388, is all that we have by this writer, but although small in quantity, it has considerable interest with regard to the growth of the notion of "Key," as opposed to the idea of "Mode." See above on this question, pp. 119, etc., 125, etc., 127-140.

Thomas Warrock was a remarkably original writer. The two pieces mentioned deserve careful attention. He shows modern tendencies of key and of harmony, besides a general smoothness quite foreign to England, the Netherlands, or even Italy.

15. *Ferdinando Richardson* (Sir Ferdinand Heyborne). 8 pieces, all Pavans and Galliards, with "variations" on them.

None of these are worth playing, in comparison with the other things in the book.

i. 27 and i. 32 are Pavan and Galliard *en suite*, and the Galliard really *is* the same tune as the Pavan, according to the recognised rule. See above, p. 114, or compare Bull's Pavan and Galliard, "St Thomas Wake," in Parthenia (quoted in "Shakespeare and Music," 201, 202).

16. *Richard Farnaby* (son of Giles Farnaby). 4 pieces. ii. 374, a "Duo." Dry and short. ii. 263, "Fayn would I wedd," a good example of simple musicianly variations on a typical melody 400 years old. (Rather like his father's "Quodling's Delight," ii. 19.)

This one page (ii. 263) is valuable to a student. In it are seen (*a*) the ancient Dorian or Æolian burden or bagpipe bass of *la sol la mi*, which can be sung with the first half of each section. (*b*) The ordinary Dorian harmonies, with the accustomed "relief" in what *we* call "the relative major." (*c*) The obvious way of the invention of "Canons," by accident. See, for instance, the melody of section 2, where each of the first three pairs of bars harmonises with the other; or, the first four bars of all three sections, which will fit together well. The latter example shows clearly how the discovery of Canon might be made.

ii. 162, "Nobody's Gigge." An excellent piece. See above, p. 46.

ii. 494, Variations on "Hanskin." The tune is associated with Shakespeare's song, "Jog on," in the *Winter's Tale*. See "Shakespeare and Music," 192, for a different version of the first half, and indeed of the whole tune. "Hanskin" is the last piece in the Fitzwilliam Virginal Book, and is numbered CCXCVII. These four pieces show Richard Farnaby to have been a man of great gifts, and a worthy son of his father.

17. *Edward Johnson.* 3 pieces. ii. 366, "Jhonson's Medley." This is really a Pavan and Galliard in one piece, with the usual variations. It has, however, other curious features, *e.g.*, the approximation to the homophonic madrigal, at the top of p. 367 (including the last chord of the previous page), and in the passage labelled 3, beginning on the fourth line of that page. ii. 436, Pavana "Delight," with Galiarda ii. 440 following, *en suite*, "set by Byrd." The Galiarda (see above, p. 115) is properly allusive of the Pavana *in all three sections*. On p. 438 is again seen the homophony already noticed in the "Medley."

18. *Francis Tregian* (who may have written out this collection in the Fleet Prison, between 1609 and 1619). i. 415, "Heaven and Earth," *may* be by Tregian. It is an ornamented version of some ecclesiastical melody (?). i. 226, This is probably *not* by Tregian, in spite of its title "Treg Ground," as in the Nevell Book it is called "Hugh Ashton's Grounde." Also, it is "set" by Byrd, so, after all, very little can be by Tregian himself.

For i. 321 and i. 327, see under Peter Philips.

Thus Tregian's name is of no importance, except as that of the possible compiler and writer of the Fitzwilliam Book.

Other names of Composers in the book are Tisdall, Oystermayre, Oldfield, Pichi, Galeazzo (of these nothing seems known). Again, Strogers, Blitheman, Rosseter, Parsons, Marchant, Hooper, Harding, are little more than mere names to us. The Italians, Caccini, Lasso, Striggio, Marenzio, whose Madrigals appear in Philips's arrangements, can hardly be considered here.

19. *John Dowland* is almost the only other well-known musician we have not yet noticed. There is, however, very little of his work in the book. One piece is the famous " Lachrymæ Pavan," which was first published in 1600, and is " set" in the Fitzwilliam book by Byrd, Farnaby, and Morley, ii. 42, 472, 173. Also see the note on "Lachrymæ," in the printed Fitzwilliam Virginal Book, ii. p. vi., and the Musical Antiquarian Society's edition of Dowland's " First Set," etc. (1597), p. 2, where the dramatic quotations alluding to it are given. It is worth playing " plain," as evidently its popularity must have been considerable.

To Dowland's name we must also add "Piper's Galliard," ii. 242 (Bull), which is simply a version of Dowland's madrigal (publ. 1597), " If my complaint " (" First Set of Songs," No. 4). Further remarks will be found above, pp. 27-30.

20. *Thomas Tallis*, the best-known name of the time, at least to modern ears. Only 2 rather dry ecclesiastical pieces, i. 427 and ii. 1. The latter is dated 1564, and is terribly long (about eleven minutes). It is almost worth playing to remind one of the unwisdom of judging a man by one specimen of his worse work (compare, perhaps, Browning's "Sibrandus Schafnaburgensis ").

21. *William Tisdall.* By whom 5 pieces (a mistake in the Index makes a Fantasia of the Galiarda): ii. 276, a good Alman, worth playing " plain"; ii. 486, Galiarda, quite

good : ii. 278, Pavana Chromatica, called "Mrs Katherin Tregian's Pavan." Seems to recognise a "Key" of E major and minor (see above, pp. 128-9); ii. 306, Pavana, "Clement Cotton," quite good; ii. 307, Pavana, Dorian transposed or (?) G minor.

22. *Edmund Hooper.* Two short dances (Index gives only *one*): ii. 309, Alman, very excellent; ii. 312, Corranto, for which see above, pp. 31 and 35.

23. *Marchant.* One piece, ii. 253, a good Allemand. He is said to have been a musician in the service of Lady Arabella Stuart, King James I.'s cousin, who died in 1615.

24. *Nicholas Strogers.* One piece, Fantasia, i. 357.

Full of queer "false relations"; but a capital piece of its kind, by a good man. See above, p. 63.

An evening service in D minor, by Strogers, was rescued by my father, John Naylor, the late organist of York Minster, from the MSS. of the Cathedral Library, and formed part of the *répertoire.*

25. *Jehan Oystermayre.* Galliard, ii. 405. A charming piece. (See above, pp. 22 and 122). I rely on this as an example of modern key effect. See sec. 2.

26. *Philip Rosseter.* ii. 450, A good Galliard, "set" by G. Farnaby. Worth playing throughout (something is wanting in bar 2).*

Rosseter published "Ayres" in 1601, and "Consort Lessons" in 1609.

27. *Parsons* (? Robert or John), ii. 135, "In Nomine." Not very interesting.

28. *James Harding.* ii. 47, Galiarda "sett foorth by" Byrd. Very good.

* In the 3rd section of this Galliard, ii. 452, top line, last bar, the 2nd, 3rd, and 4th crotchets in the left hand ought to be C D E F, as may readily be seen by comparing the four previous bars.

ADDENDA

Nicholas Strogers, see above, p. 208. The "Gostling" MS. Choir Books at York contain, besides the "service" named above, an anthem by Strogers, "O God be merciful."

Edmund Hooper, see above, p. 208. The same MSS. at York contain three anthems by Edmund Hooper (1553-1621), viz., "O Thou God Almighty," "Behold, it is Christ," and "Teach me, O Lord."

John Dowland, see above, pp. 26-30. Mr Barclay Squire's interesting article in the "Musical Times" (vol. 37, Dec. 1st, 1896) gives a curious letter from Dowland to Sir Robert Cecil, dated Nürnberg, Nov. 10, 1595, concerning the "villainy of these most wicked priests and Jesuits," and warning Queen Elizabeth to beware of them.

Mordents, and the sign for them, used in the Fitzwilliam Virginal Book, see above, pp. 32, 85, 182-3.

I find that Dr James Nares (1715-83) used the same sign for the mordent, viz. a double stroke, more or less sloping, but with this difference, that it was written *over* the note, not across the tail. The sign occurs frequently in the MSS. in the Fitzwilliam Museum at Cambridge, of organ and harpsichord music by Nares, and in the engraved copy of his "Lessons" for Harpsichord. The dates of these are marked in the handwriting of Lord Fitzwilliam, 1767 and 1768.

INDEX

A

ÆOLIAN, *see* Mode.

Allgemeine Deutsche Biographie, 22 note.

Almain, *see* Alman.

Alman, a dance, 7; 31 (Hooper's); related to Pavan and Brawl, 32, 34; Elizabethan compared with Bach, 38 ff.; related to French Branle, 41; form of, 119, 120; "key" in, 125; other examples, Anon. 131, R. Johnson 137.

"Amarilli, mia bella," Caccini's madrigal, arranged by Philips, 193-4.

Ammerbach (1571), on fingering, 158.

Anagrams, on Tabourot and Dowland, 28.

Anonymous composers, 200, best works named.

Answer (fugal), contrary motion, by Sweelinck, 61; *dux* and *comes*, 65; false answer, 67, 70 ff.; real and tonal. 72, 73 ff.

Arbeau, 15, 20-22, 25, 28; galliard, etc., 49; *also see* "Orchésographie."

Army Life, piece by Byrd, 3.

Arpeggios, in Bull's "Salvator Mundi," 181.

Arrangements for virginals, of 'services' and anthems, 2; of madrigals, 5, 6, 130 note, 169; examples, 193-6.

Ashton, Hugh, "ground" varied by Byrd, 188.

"Ay me poor heart," arrangement of G. Farnaby's canzonet, 130 note, 169, 197.

Ayres, Dowland's first book of, 29.

B

BACH, Emmanuel, fingering in "Versuche," 159.

Bach, J.S., Capriccio on the Departure of a Friend, 96; B. and "Temperament," 102-3; "key," 102; on fingering, thumb, etc., 160; predecessors (organ), 169; alteration of plain song, 186; uncertain rhythm in corantos, 201.

Bagpipe, *see* Bass; also 144, Bull's Galliard.

Baldwin, John, 2, copies "Lady Nevell's Book."

"Barafostus' Dream," 83, 84, 86, 89, 200.

Barnfield, Richard, sonnet on Dowland, 27.

Bars, irregular use of, 63, 84a, 113 note, 133c, 187.

Bass, Drone, 141-148, 205 (16).

Basse-dance, 20, 21, 49; steps of, 50.

"Bebung," on clavichord, 161.

Beethoven, 4; programme sonata, 97.

"Bells, The," romantic piece by Byrd, 5; described, 97-8.

Bevan, 2, "services" arranged for virginals.

Binary Form, 119, 126.

Bizet, *see* Carmen.

Blitheman, organ piece, 169, 177; harmonies implied in his "Gloria tibi Trinitas," 185; 207.

"Bonny sweet Robin," *see* Robin

Bourdon, Burden. *see* Bass.

Brahms, 4; development of themes, 124.

Brawl (Bransle), related to Alman and Pavan, 32, 41; Tomkins'

Brawl, 41, 201; steps of, 41; peculiar forms of, 42.

Bremner, R., and the Fitzwilliam Book, 9.

Broken octaves, sixths, and thirds, examples by Bull, 191.

Bull, Dr John, 2, 3 (Parthenia), 6 (Antwerp), 8 (modulation), 9 (Gresham Professor), 13, 21 (suite), 24, 25 and 197 (arranges madrigal); remarkable pedal, 64; subject and answer, 67; fantasia, 75, 76; "Walsingham," 86; Hexachord, 101-6; Bull's characteristics, 105, 127-8; St Thomas Wake, 115, 130; music of his "Juell," 146; his fingering, 163, 165-6; his organ pieces, 169; specimen of his "Christe Redemptor," 176-7; of his "Gloria tibi Trinitas" 178-180; his fondness for curious "proportions," 124, 178; "Sesqualtera," example, 180; "Salvator Mundi," extracts from, 181-3; his Preludes, 189-90; examples of difficult passages, 190-1; best works reviewed, 198.

Bülow, von, on fingering, 157.

Burden, see Bass.

Burney, Dr, and the Fitzwilliam Book, 9.

Byrd, William, 2 (Lady Nevell), 3 (Parthenia), 13, 24, 25, 26 (Lachrymæ), 30, 33 ($\frac{18}{4}$ time), 43 (Gigg), 48 (Lavolta); fantasias, 65; fantasias, 70 ff.; Miserere, 74; fantasia, tonal answers, 75, 77; variations on "Walsingham," 81-83; 85 ("The woods so wild"); "O mistress mine," 89; "Jhon come kisse me now," 90-92 (music and words), 125 (modern tendency); 93 (see Gibbons); "The Bells," 97; Byrd as Romanticist, 93, 98; Hexachord, 105; uses old song in "Hunt's up," 125; his characteristics, 93, 98, 105, 128 (contrasted with Bull); his fingering, 167; his organ pieces, 169, also see his "Miserere," 74; variations on "Tregian's Ground," 188; his Pre-

ludes, 189-90; best works reviewed, 198-9.

C

CACCINI, 6; his "Amarilli, mia bella," quoted, with Philips' transcription, 193-4.

"Callino Casturame," 7, 85, 87-8.

Canon, in variation by Tomkins, 189 invention of canon, 205-6.

Canto Fermo, pieces on, see Organ Music.

"Carman's Whistle, The," 125.

"Carmen," song from, with drone bass of ancient type, 144 note.

Chappell, on Fitzwilliam Book, 10; words of songs, 15, 79, 83, 88, 89, 90, 93.

"Chirping of the Lark, The," 15.

Chord passages, Bull, 165, 190.

Chords, source of, as harmony, 141-8.

"Christe Redemptor," 116; quoted, 176.

Chromaticism, 16th century; Tomkins, 18, 19d; Tisdall, 128; G. Farnaby, 99; Tallis, 174.

Cinquepace, dance; steps of, 52.

Clavichord, action and touch, 161.

"Come, Holy Ghost," see "Salvator Mundi."

Compass of virginals, 133f., 150-2, 154-5, 157.

"Conceits" in Fantasias, 59-63; mystical conceit by Philips, 62-3.

Congee, dancing term, 50 note.

Coperario, 7 note, 130 note.

Coranto (courante), 7, 15; Hooper's, 35; steps, 36; Shakespeare, 36, 37; Selden, 37; uncertain rhythm, 201.

Corrections in text of Fitzwilliam Virginal Book, 75, 147, 191, 201 notes, 202 notes, 203 (11).

"Cosi morirò," by Luca Marenzio, arranged by Philips, 193; 195.

Cosyn, Benjamin, his Virginal Book, 1, 2.

Couperin (1717), on fingering, 159-60.

Croce, Giovanni, 30; friendship with Dowland.

D

DANCES, suite of, 4; in Masque, 7, and notes; in Fitzwilliam Book, 4; classes of, 14-15; instruments used in, 20-21; dances sung, 15, 20, 55; dances named after persons, etc., 24, 25; list of useful short dances, 202.
Dannreuther's explanation of "slide" confirmed, 166-7.
"Daphne," song, 79, etc.(variations); 89-90.
Dates given, of pieces in Fitzwilliam MS., 6, 13, 25; list of such dates, 130 note; extracts from earliest dated piece, Tallis' "Felix namque," 173-6.
Development, in form, 114 ff.; sequence, 121; 124.
Dominant harmony, see Tonic; also 117, 119, 120, 125, 126, 138.
Dorian, see Mode.
Dowland, J., 24-6 (Lachrymæ), 28, 29; his life and wanderings, 26-30; madrigal arranged, 169, 197, 200; work reviewed, 207; 209.
Drum, in 16th century dance, 20.
Duet for two virginals, 199.
Duke of Brunswick's Alman, form of, 120.
Dump, an English dance, 8.
Dumpe, The Irish, 7, 8.
"Durchführung," or free section in binary form, 117, 118, 16th century example.
Dvořak, modal relics, 127.

E

EDWARDS, Richard, 8.
"Ein' Feste Burg," 116.
Elizabeth, Queen, a player on the virginals, 1, 9.
"English" fingering (1599-1757), 158-60.
Enharmonics, see Notation, Key, also 106, 127 (Bull).

F

FALKENER, Rudolph (1762), and "English" fingering, 159.
"Fall of the Leafe, The," set by Peerson, 202.
False relations; Strogers, 63, 64; Farnaby, Tallis, 68.
Fancy pieces, 16th century, 5; music of Farnaby's Dreame, 94; 94-99.
Fantasias (Fancies), fugal, 5, 57-78, 102; in Shakespeare, 59; writers of, 60; Munday's Fantasia on the weather, 96, 202; correction in "The Fantasia on the Weather," 202 note.
Farnaby, Giles; romantic pieces, 5; Maske, 7 and notes; Pavans by, 24; Galliard by, 47; setting of 'Lachrymæ,' 24 note; 25, 26, 30, 31; curious Gigue, 45; G. Farnaby's Fantasia, 67-70 (music); "Daphne," 89, 90; variations on "Daphne," 79-81; his "Dreame," 94, 98; his "Conceit," 96; his "Robin," 201; King's Hunt and Spagnioletta, etc., 125; Canzonet arranged, 130 note and 197; his variations on a ground bass, 187; prelude, 189, 192; best works reviewed, 199-200.
Farnaby, Giles and Richard, father and son, 46.
Farnaby, Richard, "Nobody's Gigge," 46, 116, 136; "Fayne would I wedd," 136, 200; work reviewed, 205-6.
"Fayne would I wedd," 136, 200, 205.
"Felix namque," plain song; set by Tallis, 173-5.
Fifths. consecutive, Byrd, 44a, Sweelinck, 109.
Fingering (1571, 1599, 1656, 1697, 1735, 1741), 158 ff., "English" and "German," 158-60; Falkener, Heck, Clementi, Dussek, 159; E. Bach, scales, 159; Couperin, examples, 159-60; E. Bach on passing of fingers and of thumb, 160; J. S. Bach on the same, 160;

examples, Munday, 162-3; Bull, 163, 165-6; Byrd, 166-167; *Anon.*, 164; von Bülow, 157; Repetition, 161; examples of, 164, 165; other examples, 162-8, 189, 190; curious use of the figures, 166-7.

Fitzwilliam, Lord, and the Fitzwilliam Book, 9.

Fitzwilliam Museum, Cambridge, 1.

Fitzwilliam Virginal Book; contents, 3 ff., 57; classes of pieces, 4, 14, 15; date of MS., 1, 6 (dates of Philips' pieces); list of dates in MS., 130 note; description of MS., 8; history of MS., 9 ff.

Flat (♭), use of, in Modal Transposition, 122, 185, *also see* Signature.

Form; external, 114-16; internal, 116-123; Binary, 117, 137; free section, 118; sequence, 121; general tendencies in 16th century, 123, 126, 138.

"Fortune," song, 85; account of, 88.

Foster, Will, his Virginal Book, 2.

France, music in, 16th century, 29, 30.

"Free" section in binary form, 117, 118, 138.

"Freno," part of a madrigal of Marenzio, arranged by Philips, 195.

Frohberger, programme music, 97.

Fugue, 5; 57-78; examples by Sweelinck, Philips, Strogers, Bull, Farnaby, Byrd, 61-78; history of the name, 58; Real, and Tonal, 71-78; on Hexachord, Sweelinck, 107-109.

Fuller, on Dowland, 28.

G

Gabrieli, organ music, 169.

Gaffurius, on "proportions," 124.

Galeazzo, composer of a Prelude, 189, 207.

Galliard; with Pavan, 4; made out of Pavan, 21, 34, 114 ff., 200 (5c), 205 (15); steps of, 21 f.; music of Oystermayre's, 22-24; "Captain Piper's," 25 f.; Galliard *en suite*, E. Johnson, 115 (music); Richardson, Bull, Philips, Byrd, 115; Morley, 200; Galliard *en suite* with Prelude and Pavan, 116 (Parthenia); Bull's, with bagpipe harmony, 144; Farnaby's, 202.

Gam-ut, 100 note.

Germany, music in, 16th century, 30.

"German" fingering (1571-1774), 158-160, etc.

Gibbons, Orlando, 2, 3, 86 and 93 (Woods so Wilde), 130 note; work reviewed, 201.

Gigue; usual form of, 42; music of Byrd's, 43-4; various forms of, by Bull, Byrd, G. and R. Farnaby, 44-46; Bull's "myselfe," 44, 95; Richard Farnaby's "Nobody's Gigge," 46, 111, 116.

Giraldus Cambrensis (end 12th century) on bémol, 146.

"Gloria tibi Trinitas," set by Bull, Parsons, Blitheman, 177; specimen of Bull's setting in $\frac{11}{4}$ time, 178-180; harmonies of Blitheman and Bull, 185; prelude to, 190.

"Go from my window," song, arr. Morley and Munday (?), 85, 90, 202; on "burden," 145.

Gray's Inn, Masque, 7, 130 note.

Graye's Galliard, Sir John, 25.

"Grounde," pieces on, 186-88; extract from Giles Farnaby, 187; Byrd's, on Tregian *or* Hugh Ashton, 188; Inglott's, 188, 203; Tomkins', 188, 201.

H

"Hamlet," *see* Ophelia.

Handel, material borrowed from previous centuries, 62; false answers, 67; Sweelinck, 108.

"Hanskin," song, 86; R. Farnaby's setting, 206.

Harding, James, 207; work reviewed, 208.

Harmonic basis; Æolian, 135, 145, 147; Mixolydian, 144.

Harmony, early Western, 141 ff. ; of 13th century, 141 f. ; connection with Drone bass, 144-148.

Harmony, growth of modern, 110-111, 118-120 ; Tisdall, 129 ; Farnaby, 133-5 ; Oystermayre, 139 ; causes alteration of plainsong, 183-4, 185, 186.

Harmony, Modal, 131-4 (music), 135-6 (music), 113 note (music) ; contrasted with key harmony, 138-9 (music).

Haye, dance ; tune and steps, 54 (for explanation of steps, see p. 50).

Hawkins, Sir J., and the Fitzwilliam Book, 9, 43.

"Heaven and Earth," Tregian's (?), 85, [? Te Deum or Sanctus], 186.

"Heigh ho, nobody at home," old catch, on burden, 142.

Hexachord, pieces on the, 4, 8, 100-110 ; Bull's, as evidence of modern modulation, 127 ; Byrd's, 127-8 ; Sweelinck's, combined with Fugue, 107-9.

Heyborne, Sir F., Pavan and Galliard en suite, 34 ; work reviewed, 205.

History of Music, The Oxford, 3, 193.

"Ho-hoane, The Irish," see "Ochone."

Hooper, 7 ; Alman, 31 ; Coranto, 35 ; key with 3 sharps, 110 ; 207 ; work reviewed, 208 ; anthems, 209.

Humorous Songs, 16th century, 90-92.

"Hunt's up," Byrd's, 125 (No. 10), 199.

I

"If my complaint," madrigal arranged by Bull for virginals, 25-6, 169.

Inglott, William, his "Galliard Ground," 188 ; work reviewed, 203 ; correction of text, 203 (11).

"In Nomine," see "Gloria tibi Trinitas."

Intonation, just, etc., 101 note, 103 and note ; also see Temperament.

Irish music in Fitzwilliam Book, 7, and see "Ochone."

"Irishe Ho-hoane, The," see Ochone.

Italian fingering, 17th century, 158.

Italy, music in, 16th century, 30.

Ionian, see Mode.

J

JENKINS, John, Fancy for viols, 102 (modulation).

"Jesu dulcis memoria," see "Christe Redemptor."

"Jhon come kiss me now," humorous song, tune and words, 90-92 ; set by Byrd, 125 (No. 1).

Jig, see Gigue.

"Jog on," Shakespeare's, see Hanskin.

Johnson, Edward, Pavan and Galliard en suite, 34 ; music of, 114-115 ; work reviewed, 206.

Johnson, Robert, Alman, 111 (example of modern key), 202 ; music of the same, 137 ; work reviewed, 202 ; correction in text, 202 note.

"Juell, Dr Bull's" (Jewel), 164, 198.

K

KEY, signs of, in 16th century, 8, 25 (four sharps, by Tisdall), 71 (fugal answers), 71 (early signatures) ; list of passages, 110-111.

Key, enharmonic change of, 102-3 ; origins of, 101, 110 f., 125.

Key, C major, 111, 125 ; G major, 119, 126 ; G minor, 126, 129 ; D major, 119, 125, 126, 138 ; A major, 31, 110 ; E major, 131 ; E or B major, 103 ; B♭ major, 110 ; E and B major, Tisdall, in relation to Mixolydian mode, 129.

Key, List of pieces shewing "key," 125-6 ; characteristics of "key" contrasted with those of "mode," 135-6, 138 ; example of absence of "key" effect, 187 ; also see Modulation.

"King's Hunt, The," G. Farnaby, 125 ; fingering, 167.

Kuhnau, Biblical sonatas, 96.

L

LA, Sol, La, Mi, harmonic basis, 135, 142.

"Lachrymæ," by Dowland, 24 and note, 25, 26, 169, 200.
Lasso, Orlando, 6, madrigals arranged.
Lavolta, method of dancing, 37; Morley's, 48; steps of, 53; old binary form, 118-119; Byrd, 126; Morley, Modern Binary, 126 (No. 17).
"Leaves be Greene, The," set by Inglott, 203, tune in bass or tenor.
Lumley's Paven, Lord, 24.
Lute, as song accompaniment, 29.

M

MADRIGALS, arranged for virginals, 4; Peter Philips' transcriptions of Lasso, Striggio, Marenzio, Caccini, 6; Bull's of Dowland, 25-6; 112; Giles Farnaby's of his own, 169; examples from Philips' arrangements, 193-6.
Maies (1741), on fingering, 158.
"Mal Sims," form of, 117 (music).
March, The Earl of Oxford's, by Byrd, 126 (No. 20).
Marchant, composer, 42, 207; account of, 208.
Marenzio, 6 (madrigal arranged); 30 (corresponds with Dowland); Philips' transcription of "Cosi morirò," 193; of "Tirsi," 195-6.
"Martin said to his man," humorous song, 90.
"Maske of Flowers," 7 note, 130 note.
Masque, dances for, 7; order of, 7 note 2; Pavan in Masque, 20; Lady Zouche's, 126.
Mattheson (1735), on fingering, 158.
"Mayden's Song, The," 199 and note.
"Micrologus" of Ornithoparcus, 27 note, 29.
"Miserere," plain song, set by Byrd, 74, 186; by Bull, 186.
Mixolydian, see Mode.
Mode; Dorian, 61 (example), 62, 122, 202; Dorian bass and harmonies, 205 (16); Mixolydian, 69 (example), 72 (example), 103;

Æolian, 70 (Byrd, fugal answers), 78 (Tallis, fugal answers), 130 note, 142 and 143 (examples), also 200, 205 (16); Ionian, 140, 200; characteristic harmonies of Mode, 111, 119, 122, 125 (Nancie), 138 (example); effect of Mode on the development of modern music, 123; "Mode" mixed with "Scale," 131-2 (example), 133e; "Mode" contrasted with "Key," 129, 138-9; Æolian harmony, 135, 136, 142-3, 185; Æolian 7th, "flat," 173; Relics of Modes surviving, 127; also see Transposition.
Modulation, enharmonic, 8, 106 (Bull).
Modulation of Key, early history of; Jenkins, 102; Bull, 105-6; Byrd, 110; Oystermayre, 111; "Walsingham," 120; Byrd contrasted with Bull, 127-8; Tisdall, 129; Oystermayre, 139.
Montegle's Pavan, Lady, 24.
Mordents in Fitzwilliam Book, 32, 85; examples from Bull's "Salvator Mundi," 182, 183; in Nares, 209.
Morisco, dance, 55; the King's, 200.
Morley, T., 2; on galliard, 21; his setting of "Lachrymæ," 24 note, 26, 200; publisher, 29; 30; on eight-bar strains, 32; on the Volte, Courante, etc., 37; Tonal "answer" in his Fantasia, 76; "Go from my window," 85; modern tendencies of key in "Nancie" and Alman, 125; modern tendencies of Modulation and Form, in Lavolta, 126; best works reviewed, 200-1.
Munday, John; "Go from my window," 26, 85; "Munday's Joy," 95; his Fantasia on the Weather, 96; fingering, 162-3; corrections in text, 201, notes; work reviewed, 201-2.
Muscadin, dance, 15; also as song, 15; variations on, 55; modern tendencies of key, 125 (No. 4); 200.
Music on the Continent, 16th century, 6, 29, 30.
"Musica Transalpina" (1588), 195.

Musical Antiquarian Society's publications, 21, 26, 30.

N

NAMES of persons, attached to Dances, 24-5; *also see* Ashton.
"Nancie," set by Morley, 125.
Netherlands, The, associated with the Fitzwilliam Virginal Book, 6, 10, 13.
Nevell's, My Lady, virginal book, 2, 188.
"Nobody's Gigge," tune quoted, 46; shewing key of C, etc., 111; shewing formal repetition, 116.
Notation of time signatures, $C = \frac{3}{2}$, 81, 82, 119, 144; $\mathbb{C} = \frac{6}{4}$, 170; $\phi = \frac{11}{4}$, 178; list of instances, 187.
Notation of enharmonics, 104, 106, 131.
Notation of "key," 31, 131-3.
"Now God be with old Simeon," introduced in Byrd's "Hunt's Up," 125 (No. 10), 199.

O

"O MISTRESS Mine," 89, 125 (Key of, contrasted with Mode in "Woods so wild ").
"Ochone, The Irish," 7, and photo of MS. facing p. 8.
Oldfield, Thomas, composer of a prelude, 189, 207.
Ophelia's songs, remains of in Fitzwilliam Book, 87, 188, 119.
"Orchésographie," Arbeau's, on the Pavan, 20; on Passamezzo, 21; anagram on name Tabourot, 28; Alman and Bransle, 32; Pavan turns into Coranto, 34; steps of Courante, 36; "simples" and "doubles," 36; Branle des Sabots, 41; Basse dance, Tordion, Galliard, Lavolta, 49-53, steps and tunes; Round, 53 and 54; the Haye, steps and tune, 54.
Organ music, 16th century, 5, 169 ff.; founded on Plain Songs, 169; names of composers, 169; examples, *Anon.* on "Veni," 170; harmonies

of the same, 171-2; extract from Bull's Fantasia on the same, 76; Tallis, "Felix namque," 173-6; Bull, "Christe Redemptor," 176-7; Bull, on "Gloria tibi Trinitas," in $\frac{11}{4}$ time; 178-180; another setting of the same, with "Sesquialtera," 180; specimens from Bull's "Salvator Mundi," 181-3; implied harmonies, Bull and Blitheman, 184-5.
Ornaments, mordents, slides, 19a, 32, 166-7, 182-3, 209.
Ornithoparcus, Andreas, 27 note, 29.
Oystermayre, Jehan, 6; his Galliard, 22; 22 note; modulation, 111; "development," 122-3; modern "key" effect, 139; 207, 208.
Oxford History of Music, 3, 193.

P

"PARSIFAL," tradition of modal harmonies, 127.
Parsons, organ piece, 169, 177, 185; 207.
Parthenia, 3; Bull's St Thomas Wake, 21; 115; 'suites' of 3 movements, 116; Pavana, Gibbons, 130 note; prelude to "Carman's Whistle," 168, 190; 201.
Part-songs, 16th century, 29.
Passamezzo (passymeasures pavan), 21; and galliard, 33, 147.
Patrons of music, 30; *also see* Names.
'Pause' chord, final, 32, 36, 95, 132-3, 137.
Pavan, associated with Galliard, etc., 4, 14; Morley, 21; Edward Johnson's, *en suite*, 114-115; 116; 200 (5 c.); related to Brawl and Alman, 32; altered to Coranto, 15; Pavan by Tomkins, 16-19, 201; by Bull, modern key effect, 125; by Bull, bagpipe tune in galliard, 144; Pavana Chromatica, by Tisdall, 103, 128-9; steps of, and manner of dancing, 20; instrumental music for, 21; "Lachrymæ" Pavan, 24, and note; Robert Johnson's, 202.
"Pawles Wharfe," in D major, etc., 111, 119, 125 (No. 12); contrasted

with modal pieces, 133; music of, 134; 199.

Pedal bass, *see* Bass.

Peerson, Martin, "The Primerose," 147, 202; work reviewed, 202.

Penna, Father L. (1696), on fingering, 158.

Pepusch, and the Fitzwilliam Book, 9, 10.

Percy's Reliques, 2, 87, 88.

"Pescodd Time." *see* "Hunt's Up."

Philips, Peter, arrangements of madrigals, 6, 169; specimens of, 193-6; Philips and "short octaves," 153; and date of Fitzwilliam Book, 13; dates of his own pieces, 130, 203; his Pavans, 25, 33; his Fantasia, 62; his Pavana Dolorosa, 203; his Passamezzo Pavan and Galliard, with Saltarello, 203; list of his original pieces, 203; best work reviewed, 203.

Pichi, an unknown composer, 207.

Piper's Galliard, Captain; arranged by Bull from Dowland's madrigal, 25 f.; 169.

Piper's Pavan, arranged by Peerson, 202.

Plain Song, harmonies set, by 16th century writers: *Anon.*, 171-2; Tallis, 173-5; Bull, 176-7, 178-80, 180, 181, 182, 183, 184, 185; Blitheman, 185.

Popular music, its influence on the classical school, 124; list of examples, 125.

Preludes, *en suite*, 4, 116; in Fitzwilliam Book, 169; account of them, 189-192; examples of technical passages; Bull, 190, 191; Sweelinck, 192; *Anon.*, 164.

"Primerose, The," set by Peerson, 202.

"Primitive Music," Wallaschek, 5.

Programme music, 16th century, 96; 17th century, 96, 97; 18th century, 96-7; 19th century, 97.

Proportion (time); Bull and Gaffurius, 124; Bull, strange combination, 178; example of "Sesquialtera," 180; relation to signatures, 187.

"Put up thy dagger, Jemy," 199.

Q

"QUADRAN" Pavan, 24.

Queen Elizabeth, 1, 9.

"Quodling's Delight," modal tune and harmony, contrasted with "Pawle's Wharfe," 125 (No. 12); not in "key" of A minor, 133-4; music of, 135-6; shows characteristics of Æolian mode, 136; compared with Rameau, 200.

R

RAMEAU (1683-1764), 47, 200.

Repetition in fingering; *Anon.*, 164; Bull, 165-6; 168 (No. 4); examples by Bull, 190 f.

Rhythmical balance in Form; "Mal Sims," 118; "Walsingham," 119.

Ricercare, 4, 58 etc., *see* Fantasia.

Richardson, Ferdinando, *see* Heyborne.

"Robin," song; in Shakespeare, 85; set by Farnaby and Munday, 86; words practically lost, 88-89; correction in Munday's, 201 note.

Romanticism, 16th century, 5; Byrd and Gibbons, "Woods so wilde," 93; G. Farnaby's "Dreame," etc., 94-5; Byrd's "Bells," 97-98; Byrd's "Walsingham," etc., 98; Farnaby's "Humour," 99; "Barafostus," *Anon.*, 201.

"Rosasolis," Farnaby's, 199.

Rosseter's Galliard, 25, 'set' by Farnaby; 208; correction in text of Galliard, 208 (26) and *note*.

Round, dance; Byrd's 'Sellinger's,' 53-4; relation to Haye or Raye, 54.

"Rowland," song; tune, 92.

S

SALTARELLA, ends Philips' Passamezzo Galliard, 33.

"Salvator Mundi," setting by Bull, 181-183.

Scale, technical passages, 191.

Scales, origin of; hexachords, 100-

101, 109; eight-note scales, 124; list of examples tending to employ modern scales, 125-6; also Byrd's Fantasia, 77; "Pawles Wharfe," 134; R. Johnson's Alman, 137.

Scales mixed with Mode, Alman by *Anon.*, 131-2 and, 133*e;* example of "keyless" ground bass, 187.

Schumann, descent from 16th century, 4.

Selden, on court dances, James I. and Charles I., 37.

Sellinger's Round, 53-54, by Byrd.

Sequence, repetition in; *Anon.*, 121; Oystermayre, 122; Tisdall, 129.

Shakespeare; "Callino castore me," 7 and 87-8; Dumps, in Lucrece, 8; Barnfield and Dowland, 27; Sir Toby on eight-bar strains in pazzamezzo, 33; Shakespeare songs in Fitzwilliam Book, 85; Ophelia's songs, "Walsingham," 86, and tune, 119; "Fortune," "Robin," "O mistress mine," 88-9.

Signature, modal; sign of "transposition," 62, not of "key," 71; signature of *two* flats for "double transposition," 104; example of "transposed" Dorian mode, with signature of *one* flat, 121-122.

Signature, time; C=$\frac{3}{2}$, 81, 82, 119, 144; 3=$\frac{6}{4}$ or $\frac{12}{4}$, 113; ¢=$\frac{6}{4}$, 170, 171; ¢ = $\frac{11}{4}$, 178; list of instances, 187.

Sinkapace, or Galliard, *see* Cinquepace.

Six-line staves for virginal music, 8, and photo. of MS. facing p. 8.

Slide, ornament, in Fitzwilliam Book, 32, 166-7.

Sonata, origin of, 4; form, 117, 119, 123.

Sol Fa, 100, 135, etc.

Songs, arranged for virginals, 4; book of songs by Dowland, 29; treatment in Fitzwilliam Book, examples, 79-93; Shakespearian, 85-89; humorous, 90; words and music of "Jhon, come kisse me now," 90-92.

Spagnioletta, dance; Farnaby's, 55,

125; Farnaby's 'Old Spagnoletta,' with modern "minor key" features, 126.

Speer, Daniel (1697), on fingering, 158.

Spohr, his chromaticisms anticipated by Tomkins and others, 19*d; see* music, p. 18.

"St Thomas Wake," Pavan and Galliard, with Prelude, *en suite*, 21; modern "key," 125 (No. 6); date, 130 note; 205 (15).

Steps of dances; Pavan and Courante, 36; Basse dance, 50; Galliard or Cinquepace, 52; Lavolta, 53; Haye, 54; Morisco, 55.

Strains; in pavan, irregular number of 'bars,' 19; ditto in galliard, 24; ditto in alman, 32*b*, 42 (list); regular strains, 32-33, 131-2, 133*b*.

Strauss, R., 4.

Striggio, madrigal arranged, 6.

Strogers, N., "services" arranged, 2; Fantasia, 63, shewing numbering of appearances of subject, and "false relations;" final bars of same, 64, shewing irregular use of bars, church music by Strogers, 208, 209.

Sub-dominant harmony, 111, 119, 125, 126, 134, 138.

Subject and answer; in Fantasia, appearances numbered, 62, 63; irregular or false, answers, 65-69, in Bull, Byrd, Farnaby, and Handel, *also see* 187; "tonal" answers result of "key," 71-73; "real" fugue in Fitzwilliam Book, 71-73; "real" fugue (1532), 73-74; "tonal" fugue, 74-78, Byrd, Bull, Morley, Tallis.

Suite, origin of, 4, 21, 114-116; possible "suite" by Morley, 200.

"Sumer is icumen in," early Western harmony, 141-2.

Sweelinck, 6; date of his "Ut, re, mi, fa, sol, la," 13; Fantasia, answer in contrary motion, 61; list of scholastic conceits in the same, 61-2; his piece on the

Hexachord, 100 ; extracts from the same, 107, 8, 9 ; 'modulation' doubtful, 129-30 ; date, as throwing light on date of Fitzwilliam Book, 130 note ; organ pieces, 169 ; prelude by, 189 ; passage from, 192 ; work reviewed,203-5; example of counter-subject derived from subject, 204c; various forms of Sweelinck's name, 204-5.

T

TABOR-PIPE, and popular music, 124.
Tabourot, see Arbeau.
Tallis, Thomas, pieces in Cosyn's Virginal Book, 2 ; his Litany, 68 ; plagal answer, 77 ; dates of pieces, 130 note ; organ pieces, 169 ; specimens of his setting of " Felix namque," 173-6 ; work reviewed, 207.
Technique, 16th century, see Arpeggio, Broken octaves, Chord passages, Fingering, Mordent, Scale ; examples, 190-192, 162-167.
Temperament, acoustical, 16th century ; enharmonic modulation, Bull, 8 ; Perronet-Thompson, 101 ; practical directions for study of "just" tuning, 101 and 102 note ; "mean-tone" tuning, 103 note ; "equal" temperament, 102 note, and 110; Bull's Hexachord as evidence, 127.
Text of Fitzwilliam Virginal Book, corrections in, 75, 111, 138, 147,164, 191, 201 notes, 202 notes, 203 (11).
Thumb, in fingering, unused in Germany and Italy, 158 ; used in England, 158-9, but R.H. avoided, 164 ; L.H. not avoided, 165.
Time, see Notation, Signature, and Proportion.
"Tirsi," Marenzio's Madrigal, arranged by Philips, 195-6.
Tisdall, W., "Pavana Chromatica" and "Pavana Clement Cotton," 25; "key" with 5 sharps, 103 ; sequence, 123 ; Mixolydian mode, and " key "with 4 or 5 sharps, 128-9; work reviewed, 207-8.

"Titus Andronicus," ballad, see Fortune.
Tomkins, Thomas ; his Pavan, 16-19 ; notes on the same, 19 ; his Hunting Galliard, 25, 201 ; his arrangement of "Barafostus' Dream," 86 (see 83), 201 ; his variations on "Up Tails All," 188 ; work reviewed, 201.
Tonal fugue, examples, 74-78.
Tonic, dominant, etc., harmony, 111, 119, 120, 125, 126, 138.
Tordion, dance, 49 ; galliard par terre.
Touch, on virginals, etc., 161.
"Tower Hill," Farnaby's, 126 (No. 19), 199.
Toye, dance, 47 ; four examples named, 202.
Transcriptions for virginals, see Arrangements.
Transposition, of modes, 62, 103 ; "double" transposition, 104 ; 122 ; Thomas Warrock's signature considered, 140 ; Æolian transposed, 185.
Tregian, F., family history of, 10-13 ; possible connection with Fitzwilliam Book, 13-14 ; Mrs K. Tregian, 25 ; Sybil Tregian (?), 10 ; Mr Tregian as copyist, 47 ; as composer, 85, 186, 206-7.
Tritone (augmented 4th) in 16th century, 171, 184.
Tuning, see Temperament.

U

"UP TAILS ALL," set by Farnaby, 188 ; variations on, by Tomkins, 188-9 ; Farnaby's, 199.
Ut, re, mi, fa, sol, la: date of Sweelinck's, 13 ; settings by Sweelinck, Byrd, Bull, Farnaby, 100-110 ; 'modulation' a 'result' of this subject, in Sweelinck and Farnaby, 129-30.

V

VARIATION form in 16th century, 4 ; variations on songs and dances, 57, 79 ; specimens, variations on "Daphne," by G. Farnaby, 79-81 ;

on "Walsingham," by Byrd, 81-83; on "Barafostus' Dream," *Anon.*, 83-84; on "Woods so wild," by Byrd, 113, *see* 145-6 for the tune; melody in tenor, 80, 84; melody in bass, 81, 188, 203 (Inglott); melody within the chords, 82; method by *agrémens*, 113; unusual method, Byrd, 113 note; "variation" leads to true "development," 124; variations on a "Grounde," by G. Farnaby, W. Byrd, W. Inglott, T. Tomkins, 187-9; specimens of Tomkins' variations on a "ground," 188-9.

"Veni," plain song; set by *Anon.*, 170; reduction of the harmony, 170-2; the same set by Bull, 76.

Verdi, and tradition, 127.

Verstegan, Richard, and Tregian, 10.

Viol da gamba, as accompaniment for song, 29.

Virdung (1511), on virginals, 150 note.

Virginal Books, 1-3.

Virginals; account of the instrument, 149-157; case of, 150, and *frontispiece*; compass of, 132, 133 f.; variety of compass, 150-1, 155, 157; jacks, and action, 150; methods of fingering, 157-168; "short octaves," 151-155; split keys, 156-7; "touch," 161; *also see* plate facing p. 149.

W

WAGNER, anticipation of, 82; tradition in, 127.

Wallaschek, "Primitive Music," 5.

"Walsingham"; in Lady Nevell's Book, 2; Byrd's variations on it, 81, 82; in Shakespeare, 85, 86, 87; the Shrine, 86; words of the songs, 86, 87; plain tune and words, 119-120; set by Bull and Byrd, 120.

Ward, John, Elizabethan composer, 2.

Ward, 1740, "Lives of the Gresham Professors," 9, 190.

Warrock, Thomas (1586); ? B♭ major, 110; ? minor chords in major key, 139-40; his two flats not a sign of "double transposition," 140; work reviewed, 205.

Wasielewski, on 16th century instrumental music; fugal answers (1532), 73, 74.

Weelkes, "services" arranged for virginals, 2.

"Well tempered Clavier," anticipated, 8, 102.

"When a liv'd at yam," Northern Song on Burden, 143.

"Why aske you," song, set by *Anon.* and G. Farnaby, 86.

Wilson, of Scarborough (1791), pianoforte by, 151.

"Woods so wild, The"; in Lady Nevell's Book, 3; set by Byrd and Gibbons, 85-6; modal harmony, 125 (No. 11); variation on, 113 note; music of, 145-6; 201.

"Woody Cock," Farnaby's, 199-200.

Wooldridge, H. Ellis, editor of Chappell, 15, 79.

Y

YORK Minster Library, MSS.; of John Jenkins' Fantasias for strings, 102; of service in "D minor" by Nicholas Strogers, 208; of anthem by Strogers, 209; of three anthems by Edmund Hooper, 208, 209.

Z

ZOUCHE's Maske, Lady, 126 (No. 18). Zumpe (1766), pianoforte by, 150.